AVENTURA, AMOR Y TACOS

The Path to Reconnecting with the Motherland

MAIRA HERNÁNDEZ

CONTENTS

Aventura, Amor y Tacos:

The Path to Reconnecting with the Motherland

Copyright © Maira Hernández, 2019

www.mairahernandez.com

All rights reserved. No part of this book may be reproduced in any form without permission in writing from the author. Reviewers may quote brief passages in reviews.

Published 2019

DISCLAIMER

No part of this publication may be reproduced or transmitted in any form or by any means, mechanical or electronic, including photocopying or recording, or by any information storage and retrieval system, or transmitted by email without permission in writing from the author.

Neither the author nor the publisher assumes any responsibility for errors, omissions, or contrary interpretations of the subject matter herein. Any perceived slight of any individual or organization is purely unintentional.

Brand and product names are trademarks or registered trademarks of their respective owners.

Cover Illustration by Gloria Felix

http://gloriafelix.com

❀ Created with Vellum

DEDICATION

Para mis abuelos, mi Amá y Apá and all those who came before me.

SI SE PUEDE!

"We need to help students and parents cherish and preserve the ethnic and cultural diversity that nourishes and strengthens this community— and this nation."

— Cesar Chavez, Civil Rights Activist

I t was a nice and sunny day with a cool breeze, typical for Bay Area weather. I was making my way up a hill in Berkeley, CA, and I was wearing stiletto pumps. How was this a good idea? After what seemed like the hike of the century, my whole family and I finally made it up to the Greek Theater at the top of the hill and through the crowded venue to our seats. I was sitting next to both of my parents in the outdoor theater filled with people all in happy spirits for this celebratory day. In all the chatter, I noticed that my dad, who was sitting to my right, was talking to the man next to him about a soccer game. My dad doesn't really watch soccer all that much, which is why I found it strange that he was going on and on about the sport. I'd like to think that both these men were talking about soccer and trying to continue the small talk to keep their emotions in check because this was a special day. Both of their kids were graduating from college!

I was graduating from UC Berkeley, the first in my family to go to college, and I had made it. This was it! This is what I had been working for all these years. This was what both of my parents had encouraged me to do, to get an education so that I wouldn't have to do the back-breaking work that my parents had. *"Es mejor trabajar con la mente que con las manos,"* my dad would always say— it's better to work with your mind than with your hands. That is the reason I always studied hard, and that was the reason we were all sitting here on this day. I was graduating from one of the best universities in the world, all to make the sacrifice my parents made when they left their country worth it. There was a moment that day sitting in the sea of people where I thought to myself, I made it! If I made it here, then I could literally make it anywhere.

This ceremony was more than a graduation. It was a cultural event! It was bilingual, catering to those who supported us through the whole journey. They played all the tunes both the graduates and our families would dance to at family parties. As graduates, we got a chance to pick two people to walk the stage with us. For me, it was my mom and dad. For others, it was their kids, significant other, or grandparents. What more perfect way to honor our success than by including those who paved the way for us? If it wasn't for my parents migrating to California, there is no way that I would have found myself walking across the stage with both of them holding my hands and waving them up in the air as if I had just won a boxing championship.

This is how I received my bachelor's degree, with my *zarape* graduation sash around my neck representing my culture, my parents with a Cal sash representing the university, all three of us walking the stage to receive a degree from one of the most prestigious universities in the country. My parents beaming with pride as we walked across the stage and I overwhelmed with emotion that I had actually done it. This was it. I had done it! I had finally proven that their migration was worth it— that coming from the *rancho*, to the hood, and to a university was possible.

I had finally made my parent's American Dream come true; they would finally have a college degree to hang up in the living room as a proud symbol of their and their child's hard work. An opportunity they never had for themselves. I did it for them, because they deserved it after all the sacrifices they made for us. They sacrificed their motherland by leaving it behind, they sacrificed their life by working hours and hours in laborious jobs, they even took a back seat when they realized there was not much they could help us with in our path through academia, and trusting that we knew what we were doing. This was understood in the crowds of people that joined us in that graduation: that somehow we created a miracle and we were all there to celebrate it; that even though most of us were strangers, we were also family because we understood each other. This dream wasn't meant for us, but here we were! It was beautiful to see the celebration, people dancing as they made their way up the stage, people chanting each other's names, flags of various Latin American countries being waved in the air, and smiles all around that lit up the evening. The whole venue beamed with joy. *¡Sí se pudo!*

Soon after that, reality struck. Without any guidance, it took months for me to land a full-time job. It then took me a couple of years to move on to a decent salaried job and a couple of years more to move to a job where my parents understood what I actually did. It was five years after graduation when I finally felt I had a good foundation in my career. The job I had was a good job. I was independent. I had health insurance and a 401K. I was living in an apartment paying rent and my bills, and my credit score was amazing. I was going on nice vacations, and I even had money in my savings account. I was doing everything perfectly, as I had been taught to do. If you compare my life at this stage to that of my parents during my same age, you could say I was doing quite well financially, given that I didn't have any kids and I was just providing for myself. I remember as a kid we use to buy milk and cheese with food stamps, shop at the swap meet, and if we needed new clothes, my mom, who was a seamstress in México, would make it for us. I was in a place where I could afford anything I needed. For my parents who came from a poor town in México, that was all they wanted for their kids.

Even then, it felt like something was missing. I realized that, in the grind, I wasn't spending that much time with family. I wasn't even spending much time with myself— you know, doing something good for the soul. It was mostly work, come home, Netflix and Chill. The weekends were about going out with my friends, dancing the night away, weekend getaways, a few interesting dates here and there. Still, something felt like it was missing. I had internalized society's view of an independent woman, self-sufficient, intelligent, hard-working, with a group of girlfriends who were just the same. I was so busy trying to prove myself to a society that continually told me that my kind of lifestyle wasn't meant for me, and I continuously pursued it to prove society wrong, which is why I didn't understand what was missing.

That is when I started to pay attention and reflect on those times I felt really connected with life. I recognized how grounded I felt when I was living at home. Granted, it was still a struggle because of the independence I held for so long, and having to slightly let go of it while living with my parents again made it a little difficult— but I was lucky to have a place to go when I was in transition. I remember during the short time I lived at home in between jobs, I would love coming home to a home-cooked meal, having my mom cook for us because that was the way she expressed her love. I would spend time with my little sister and annoy her, knowing that no matter how annoying I was she would still love me. I would also visit my niece and nephew more often and spend time with them making them laugh, asking them questions, and talking about anything from butterflies to volcanos— innocent conversations that made you realize how nice it was to talk to someone who didn't carry any stress.

Being at home made me available for family parties where there was always good food and music. I loved these times with family and cousins when all we did was drink a beer and laugh about whatever the conversation was. It's these times where we would spend the day clowning on each other and reminisce the times when we were younger. It's also during these times when my *tíos* and *tías* would ask what new adventure I had coming up because they were happy to see me exploring the world in a way they never could in their youth. These times were always filled with plenty of laughter, good food, and drinks— but it had been a while since I had done this. I was more concerned with my busy work schedule and connecting with those who understood my professional experiences that I often forgot to make time for moments like these.

I started to think back more and more, and I remembered during college orientation one of the presenters told the audience of parents to hold back on calling us, the students, too often as that would make us more homesick. At that time, I was in a place where I was craving so much independence that I took that and ran with it, and so did my parents. They didn't know any better— this whole college thing was as new for them as it was for me— so that's how it was. I spent most of my years in college only calling them about once a week. Meanwhile, I spent my whole first semester craving connection with someone who looked like me. My mom once told me that at night before she would go to bed she would often picture me going to sleep in my top bunk in my dorm, inches away from the ceiling, praying that I would be ok. Those were probably the moments where she wanted to call but didn't.

What the presenter at orientation failed to understand was that in the audience there were some people like me— the minority, who would struggle with not only being homesick but also with culture shock. I had come from a predominately Hispanic neighborhood in LA to the complete opposite where Latinos only accounted for about ten percent of the student population. I remember seeing a brown person pass by and in my mind thinking "be my friend" because at that time I was too shy to strike up a conversation. During my first semester I didn't even really know about the different resources and spaces for people like me. My only concept of college was what I saw on TV and the movies that included being best friends with your roommate and going to all the frat parties, and that did not reflect my own experience.

After my first semester I found spaces that made college feel a little bit like home and I started to rely on resources to help me deal with the whole college experience as a first-generation student. I began to believe that the only people who would understand what I was going through were the ones going through the same experiences, first-generation college students. Looking back at it now, I wish I had recognized that my struggle with culture-shock, homesickness, and being a minority in college was the same struggle my parents experienced coming to this country. I was only in college for a few years, they uprooted their whole lives and made a permanent change to a new country. Understanding that back then would have probably encouraged me to call my parents more often. To ask them how they dealt with being a minority in a new country, how they managed dealing with culture-shock and homesickness. I didn't recognize it then, so instead I made new friends. I joined new communities, and I didn't realize that, in a way, I started to replace the ones that I had left behind— not fully but enough to not notice that I was separating from my roots.

This continued through my professional career. I felt that only the people with the same kind of professional experiences as me could help me along the way, especially when climbing the career ladder. This was, I dare say, even more difficult to navigate because with college I knew the end goal was graduation, but with my career, I wasn't so sure. I kept hearing climb the career ladder, continue to increase your salary, look out for yourself, network. This was a struggle because logically I understood this concept, but it was conflicting with a lot of the values I was raised to believe in. I was raised with values of caring for your family, supporting each other in community, caring for those in need, doing and fighting for what's right.

On the other hand, I had student loans, so the most logical thing to do was to continue going on the path known by American culture as one to financial success— all while trying to hold on to the values I had. It seemed like I was playing a tug-of-war with two sets of conflicting values, and all of this made me feel like I was settling outside of myself, outside of what I have been raised to be. It was not necessarily a bad thing because continuing to succeed in a career is an accomplishment to celebrate, but I didn't feel aligned with the way I was doing it, and I didn't know why. I began to wonder if my cultural identity fit in the professional setting I was in, but my cultural identity was never something I was willing to give up. What was even more bizarre to me was

7

that I used my cultural identity in all of my jobs to relate to the people I was serving, and even then, I was feeling this way. I worked predominantly with Latinos, encouraging students to pursue education, talking to parents and introducing them to resources for their children. If I was working with predominantly Latino communities and I was good at it, why did I still feel so conflicted in the office space? Where did that leave me?

That's the thing about being the first. You're the trailblazer, and you don't know what's acceptable and what isn't, and you spend most of your time trying to figure it out. Can I wear my natural hair at the office? Can I give a friendly hug to my coworkers? Can I be all up in the *chisme* without it being an issue? Was that a racially charged statement, or am I being too sensitive? It's the struggle of proving yourself worthy of success where ever you are but also not losing sight of the identity you grew up with. We spend so much of our time trying to prove ourselves, and the effects of imposter syndrome are present everywhere. Oftentimes we think we are adjusting to success in the office, but while doing that, how much of our cultural identity do we lose, consciously or unconsciously? We often spend so much of our time code-switching from who we are authentically and how we talk around friends and family, to the professionalism we showcase in the office. It's confusing and frustrating dealing with a dual cultural identity in this country.

We come to question if we can be fully American having been raised as children of immigrants with a different language and different culture, a culture we're proud of. On the other hand, can we fully identify with our ethnic background having grown up in America with a melting pot of cultures and having lost a little bit of our own in the process? I didn't have a clear answer for this, and I had in mind that perhaps a trip to México would help me reconnect.

This is something that I still struggle with, but with the epiphanies I had in México, I now have a new perspective that helps me navigate this, whereas before I had felt completely lost. My new perspective is tied to both of my identities, one wherein they need each other to fully function. Before I was sadly paying more attention to one aspect of my identity over the other because I thought it would help me be more successful. Strangely enough, I was able to recognize how tapping into both of my identities would help me unleash a new found confidence and perspective of seeing the world and my place in it.

"We cannot seek achievement for ourselves and forget about progress and prosperity for our community... Our ambitions must be broad enough to include the aspirations and needs of others, for their sakes and for our own.
It is not enough to teach our young people to be successful... so they can realize their ambitions, so they can earn good livings, so they can accumulate the material things that this society bestows. Those are worthwhile goals. But it is not enough to progress as individuals while our friends and neighbors are left behind."

— Cesar Chávez, Civil Rights Activist

🌾 2 🌿

NO MAS RECORRIENDO EL MUNDO

"Y soy como las gaviotas,
Que vuelan de puerto en puerto.
Yo sé que la vida es corta, al fin que también la debo.
El día que yo me muera, no voy a llevar me nada.
Hay que darle gusto al gusto,
La vida pronto se acaba."

— Carlos Coral, *Un Puño de Tierra*

When I was a kid, I remember jumping into the back of our burgundy family van. It was one of those large rectangular vans that had the double doors in the middle. To me it seemed like it was a hotel on wheels because the back seat unfolded to form a bed. This was the van we took on yearly road trips down to México during the Christmas holiday, trips that would take almost two days, my mom and dad taking shifts driving down through different states in México. My aunts and uncles following along, sometimes four cars following down the road behind us. Each car with a walkie talkie where we would communicate if someone needed to make a pitstop— all of us watching out for each other, and us kids looking out through the back windows to wave hello to whoever was following us and making sure we didn't lose anyone. This was our yearly tradition, and not just in my family, but also the dozens and dozens of families we saw on the road with luggage tied at the top of their vans and trucks as they drove down those same *carreteras* to go back and visit family for the holidays.

When I say hotel on wheels, that's exactly what it was because we only slept in the van during those road trips— surviving off canned tuna, saltine crackers, cup-o-noodles, and the small thermo that connected to the car port to warm up water for our *sopa de vaso*. When I was about ten, my dad upgraded us to a similar van, green with silver stripes that had a VHS player, limo lights in the ceiling, and curtains in the windows to block out the sun. I remember vividly as my dad would pack all our luggage and tie it to the top of the van, wrapping it and securing it with rope, making it look like we were moving with all the stuff we were carrying. With a family of seven going to México for three weeks at a time, of course we carried a mountain of luggage, especially with the extra clothes we packed that we would give away to the people who needed it in the *rancho*.

December was always my favorite time of the year and I remember being excited when we were nearing our winter break and preparing to leave school for the holidays. Being in México during Christmas break meant collecting candy from all of the *piñatas* at the *posadas* and visiting our *abuelos* who would always let us buy anything from the *tienditas*— chips, ice cream, candy— we would eagerly visit these stores every day just to spend the *pesos* we had. All the *gusgueras* were that much better because they were Mexican, you know: the lollipops with the chili powder, the spicy chips, the Mexican ice cream which I dare say is comparable to gelato. Back in the day, we could only get these snacks in México because not too many stores carried them in the U.S., which meant we bought candy every day to stash for the rest of the year, even if it didn't last us that long.

Going to México also meant seeing my cousins who didn't live in California. If you know anything about Mexican families, is that they know how to reproduce. These trips were our family reunions, as *primos*, we would all be gathered in a pack, sometimes around a fire at night burning fireworks, my favorite were *cebollitas*, which we would light up and hold in between our fingers until the wick burned out and we threw them towards the sky as they flew spinning and letting out sparks into the night. In the daytime, we would make multiple trips to the *tienditas* or spend our time out in the *cancha*, the basketball court playing games, our *Tía Angelina* always coming with us to keep a watchful eye on us. These days were filled with laughter and imagination with our *primos*, sometimes even a fight or two broke out, but we always made up because we were family. Other times we would die laughing from the accidents that would happen, like my *prima* slipping into a creek of water and coming out covered in mud or getting hit in the face by the swinging piñata. I even vaguely remember someone getting married with a veil made from toilet paper. It was such a carefree time for us, when we would go with pails to the well and take drinking water in buckets back to the house or hike up the *cerro* and get *leña* for our nightly *lumbradas*— fires that we would make every night right by the front door of the house, using the wood or left over corn husks to keep the fire going just like many of our neighbors who sat around a fire every night for a chat. This is what my childhood was like in México and it was great one. I still remember getting back to the states, and our clothes would smell like México, the smell of the *rancho*, the smell of earth and fire, the smell of *tierra mojada*.

I never attributed my travel bug to my family's long road trips to México. I attributed it all to my curiosity to learn. But reflecting on these moments, I know now that my curiosity to travel came from these experiences. I always loved the idea of traveling, and when I was thirteen, I went on my first trip without my family. I went to the east coast of the U.S. with a group of students from my middle school to learn more about American history. I told my parents I wanted this trip instead of a *quinceañera*. I was never one to have a huge party and have everyone's attention directed at me. I preferred to travel, so my parents made it happen. Looking back at it now, I'm not exactly sure how they paid for it, but they made it happen nonetheless. I went to Washington D.C., Philadelphia, Virginia, New York— happy that I was the first in my family to venture off to these new cities. But when I called my mom from a pay phone that first night, I cried. That was the first time I experienced homesickness.

Several years after, I set off on my own adventure and moved away for college, far away according to my parents'— from Southern California to Northern California. I was again the first one in my family to venture off on my own to an unknown place where I knew only a couple of friends. That first year in college was also the last year that we drove down to México as a family. Now instead of the Chevy Van from the 90s, we had a Sienna minivan with a DVD player newly installed for the road trip ahead of us. This time around, before we crossed the border into México, my dad gave my siblings and I a hundred dollars each to hide in our shoes in case something happened. During those years in 2008, everyone heard a lot of terrible news from México about drug trafficking, violence, and kidnapping. Thankfully, nothing happened to us, but it was a reminder that during those years the violence in México resulted in thousands of deaths. It was eight years before I finally went back to México. My parents continued to go, but not wanting to take the risk they flew. I was too busy with school, then studying abroad, and after that working and going on vacations to even consider going back to the *rancho*. My wanderlust was so strong that I would not consider using my vacation on places I had already visited. I was creating my life, and after so many years of not returning, I thought I had in some way outgrown México because I had a career now. Wasn't my career and education the reason my parents had left México?

This isn't something I gave too much thought. What I thought about was how I was proving my success. I was hard-working enough to have graduated from one of the top universities in the country. As I started my career, I managed to get better and better jobs. I was just living life like it was expected of me: get an education, get a career, save for retirement, and take a vacation— if it's approved. Traveling had always been an escape for me, it was and still is the way I connect to life and the rest of the world, so I always made it a priority. I was so good at traveling that at one point I was traveling somewhere at least once a month— Vegas, Florida, Arizona, San Francisco, Tijuana. *No mas recorriendo el mundo.* That is all I wanted to do, travel as often as I could. Even if just for a weekend escape!

For most of these trips, that is exactly what it was, a weekend escape from life. I can't count how many times I used sick days to take a weekend trip with friends. The thrill of it all made up for the mundane feeling in the routine of life. I came to a point where I got a job that made it difficult to take these weekend trips or even a real, relaxing vacation. The amount of commitments and deadlines I had and the lack of flexibility to go off on a real adventure sucked the life out of me. I got to travel for work to a lot of less than exciting places, and I always tried to make the best of it. But there were plenty of times when I was out for work in the middle of nowhere, laying in my hotel bed crying myself to sleep for no reason at all. I was alone and lonely, working myself to death for a job that was only paying my rent and my student loans, that didn't leave enough time to sleep, visit my family, even go on a date or at the very least go to therapy.

What I can say about this job is that with all the hours I spent traveling for work, I was able to reconnect with reading. I started to listen to audiobooks on my drives and started to recognize that I was depressed— maybe not clinically depressed but, high-functioning depressed. It was the kind where I always got up on time to go to work, but just barely, and I managed to be pretty productive while flashing a fake smile, and made my way back home just to spend the evenings watching Netflix and the weekends catching up on sleep; the kind where I mostly ate scrambled eggs for dinner or a bowl of cereal because I had no energy to cook a decent meal; the kind where I couldn't be bothered with anyone else's problems because I felt like I had too many of my own. The audiobooks that I would listen to finally made me realize that I wasn't happy in life. Most of these books, written by therapist, gave me so much insight into my own self-aware- ness that I would spend hours crying on the road dealing with all my emotions— literally, driving down the I-5 ugly crying as I made my way to the next city. But thankfully, on the other side of this, I also had the books that helped me see a different kind of life. A life of happiness.

Being the adventurer that I am, I always gravitated to memoirs of those who went off and found themselves on an adventure: *Eat, Pray, Love; Top Five Regrets of the Dying; Into the Wild.* I dreamt of going on an adventure like that, but I always talked myself out of it because I couldn't quit my job when my parents came to this country for me to be successful. That was always my excuse, so I kept on with my routine: eat, sleep, work, ask for a vacation and pray it's approved. It was in 2016, eight years after my freshman year in college when I finally got a chance to visit México again during the Christmas break. This was during a particularly difficult time at work where I knew I needed to disconnect, and the one thing I remembered about the *rancho* was that it was the perfect place to do that. No wi-fi, no TV, just country. Sadly, I spent the entire week I was there in bed with the flu, but I loved being back in my *abuelos'* house and I knew that I was going to come again the next year to have a do-over because I didn't get to enjoy it like I wanted to.

It was now nearing the end of 2017, the movie *Coco* had just come out, and to say that the movie had an influence on me to go back to México would be an understatement. I still remember crying when the Disney castle came on the big screen in the movie theater during the introduction of the movie. There was *mariachi* music playing as the flags at the peaks of the Disney castle waved in the wind and the fireworks lit up the sky. Was I really already crying? YES! I was. It brought memories of the time I spent living in Florida when I would go to Disney's Epcot just to hear the *mariachi* play in front of the pyramids in little México to remind me of home. But more than that, the movie itself provided the experience of finally seeing a representation of my culture and my family on screen, from the *abuela* always making sure there was enough food on everyone's plate to being chased with the *chancla* and the love of *rancheras* to the hardcore importance of family values. It might not be a surprise to say that I almost cried the entire movie as I saw each and every one of those moments being played out because it felt like that was me. I was so in love with the movie that I made sure to book a trip again to México that Christmas break, this time staying with my *abuela* and recognizing how much of the bright colors of México were represented in the movie. So much so that I was wondering if I had seen my grandma's *colcha* in a scene of the movie, it wasn't in the movie, but the bed spread was a similar style.

That one-week trip to México was the best thing I could have asked for, during one of the most stressful times of the year. It made me recognize how at peace I was. I woke up peacefully and not to the sounds of an alarm, but rather to the smells of food in the kitchen and my *abuela* calling us to come and eat. I was eating the best food— farm to table. Being in my *abuela's* house with my sister reminded me of all our childhood memories of running around in her house and eating all the candy and chips from her store and playing cashier as we helped her with customers. I remember feeling at peace in my body, my body felt light. I no longer had that feeling of tightness at the pit of my stomach that all the stress from work had created. I was relaxed and loving every single moment of it.

During those few days, I remember looking outside the window into my grandma's vibrant aqua-green patio and noticing the bright sun, the colorful flowers, and the warmth my grandma's kitchen provided and turning to my sister and saying, "You know I could stay and live here."

She replied, "Me too."

At the time I don't think she knew how serious I was, but that might have been the moment that planted the seed to my adventure.

Our week in México went by too fast. Before I knew it, it was the first of January, and we had our flight out that night. I was so upset that work was not approving any more days of vacation because of deadlines we had to meet. This meant that I was going to miss the *fiestas* from our *rancho*. We were lucky enough that our flight didn't leave until the evening and we got a chance to dress as *guares*, like the indigenous women in Michoacán, for the first time in almost ten years— just like we did when we were kids. We wore our flower-embroidered shirts and our long heavy skirts that opened up like flowers in bloom when we twirled to the sound of the music. We got dressed and ran outside when we heard the sound of the *banda* and the fireworks calling for everyone to come out of their homes. I felt like a little girl again as we twirled in our skirts dancing our way through the *rancho* every now and again making our way under the tunnel of intertwined *rebozos* created by all the ladies as we danced in our lines with the *banda* following close behind.

The only thing different this time around was that we were pounding tequila as they passed the bottle around while yelling *"Esas Guares!?"*

And all the ladies would respond in unison with an excited "Woooooooo!" lasting a little too long given the amount of tequila we were consuming, all while having all the fun in the world!

We had a blast that morning and we were sad to leave the party early to head to the airport. We literally only had time for our last meal in México, *caldo de pollo*, and then we were on our way to the airport rushing with our outfits still on going through airport security looking like *La India Maria*. We missed the *toros*, the rodeo, from our own *rancho*. How could we miss the *toros* when we had so many memories of these traditions and our dad recording them with his old camcorder?! All because of my job. I asked myself then: did I really want to stay at a place that wouldn't even give me the flexibility to celebrate my own family traditions? The answer was a clear no, but I still went back to work and back to the routine.

It was now April, a few months after México when I had a huge wake up call. I was just off of work, and I was driving to Costco to fill my car up with gas. It was a hot day in California hitting triple digits— not sure if that has anything to do with what happened next, but it might. I remember on my drive I smelled something funny, like burned rubber. It was rush-hour in LA, so I figured it was just the traffic. This is the one reason why I forever will be grateful for the long lines at the Costco gasoline stations. Thanks to those lines I was stopped by the entrance. It was then that a woman suddenly came yelling through my passenger window. I couldn't hear her, so I slowly rolled down my window. Turns out she was trying to tell me that my car was on fire!

Confused, I put my car in park and ran to the front where she was pointing and sure enough, MY CAR WAS ON FIRE! I ran towards the pump in a panic trying to find the attendant and yelling, "Fire! There's a fire!". Realizing that this would probably cause a panic, I changed my call for help to "I need a fire extinguisher!". In those moments, as I ran back to my car a man come up and asked if I had a sweater or a blanket, so he could try to tamp the fire down. Thankfully a few seconds later, the attendant came running with a fire extinguisher and safely put it out. It turned out to be an electrical fire coming from the passenger's side headlight.

Seeing the bumper partially melted, plastic dripping on the floor, and realizing that if that woman hadn't gotten out of her car and stopped me when she did, I would have driven next to the pump with a burning car and probably exploded us all. That was the reality check I needed. I was so grateful for the woman, and the man that came and tried to help in what could have been a very dangerous situation, and that there was an attendant prepared enough to put out the fire completely. The managers came out and pointed out that I was about ten feet away from driving over the underground gasoline reservoir. It could have been a tragedy!

I was still in shock of the whole event but recognizing that by the grace of God nothing tragic happened had me on a gratitude high that I can't even describe. I called my parents and told them what happened, and while I waited for the tow truck, I called some of my friends. After I got over the shock, I just started laughing hysterically while on the phone with my a friend because it didn't make sense how I was still alive. How lucky was I that I was stopped where I was? How lucky was I that the only damage was on my car? And how hilarious was it that I can now say "I once drove into a gas station with my car on fire and survived!". Thank you, Jesus!

It was then that I began to realize it had been a long time since I had been really happy. There's nothing like a near-death experience to make you realize how happy you are to be alive. My car was out of commission, and I could have died but I was still alive! That evening, as I waited for the tow truck, I looked at the sky and saw the beautiful pink hues of the sunset and how the palm trees looked with that back-ground of colors as a group of birds flew across the sky. It had been a long time since I had paid attention to the sky in this way. I also found myself wondering if the guy with the fire extinguisher was cute, or if I was just super grateful that he saved my life. These are all thoughts that went through my mind while I waited for the tow truck to arrive with a new found appreciation for life.

Soon enough with all the books I was reading, I started to get more into inspirational books rather than the ones that helped me self-analyze my issues. Little by little, I started to realize that these authors were speaking my language of adventure, freedom, love and connection. I began to think that maybe my ideas of adventure weren't so out there, that maybe I was the one that had settled for my own current life of mediocrity. I also began to question why all these adventure books were written by white women? Could I not go on my own little adventure and represent women of color?

I watched *Eat, Pray, Love* again, and just a couple of weeks after my near death experience, I bought a one-way flight to San Juan, Puerto Rico with the intention of quitting my job that summer and spending a few months traveling and going back to México. The ticket was for accountability, so I had a date in which I had to quit my job. As soon as I made that decision, the decision to LIVE, everything started shifting in my life. I started to notice the birds chirping on my walk to the office. I started to enjoy my walks during my breaks as I felt the sun warm on my skin and as I noticed the different hues of greens in the grass and the trees surrounding me. I started taking picnics outside during my lunch break which helped me appreciate being in nature. I started to enjoy work, because I knew it was only temporary as I had committed to the decision to leave.

I began to decide what I wanted for myself, and it was happiness. Then I started to figure out what that looked like for me and what would help me get there. With that, I began having conversations about my needs. When I realized that the current environment I was in was not going to help, I knew without a doubt that it was time to move forward. If I stayed, I would have to take full responsibility for my own misery and I could not make the mistake of blaming someone else. I was tired of being tired, and I knew the one thing that truly made me happy was traveling— the kind of travel where you immerse yourself into a new environment and are open to learning from all of the new experiences that place will offer, the kind where you are forced to rely on the kindness of strangers, and the one where you realize there are kind people everywhere, the one where you are forced out of your comfort zone and you're forced into new depths of your own human experience.

The day finally came when I had to put in my two-weeks' notice, and this was probably the hardest thing I ever had to do. I spent that entire day spinning in my anxiety. I had planned to do it first thing in the morning, somehow, I put it off until it finally hit 4:45 p.m., and I started to think— Well staying another year won't be so bad, will it? As soon as I caught myself thinking this, I got up off my chair and walked over to put in my notice. I didn't feel prepared to have this conversation, but I knew if I didn't do it then I would just continue to push it off. I knew with certainty that I was not going to be happy if I stayed, so off I went. Surprisingly, the conversation went great, and in those moments, I began to feel the liberation of finally going after what I really wanted in life, the freedom of finally using my voice! The world didn't collapse like I thought it would, quite the opposite. Once I went for what I really wanted, everyone around me was extremely supportive. Just like that it was done, and there was no going back.

Everything that happened afterward was a journey. From coming to terms with the decision I had just made, to feeling the stress I held onto for so long drift away from my body with every wave as I floated in the Caribbean in Puerto Rico, to finally making it to México and struggling with the idea of actually living there for a few months and overcoming that fear, to being open to everything México had to offer, and finally to finding my peace and joy in the grace of just being the most simple version of myself and being happy. The time I spent in México was the most defining and transformative time in my life. Everything from the way I carry myself to how I share my family history, what I teach to the next generation, the way I see México, and the way I see the world has changed. It's almost as if I discovered a secret and all I want to do is share it with the world.

Traveling has always been a part of my heart, I realize now that I got my travel bug from my parents. It started the moment they decided to immigrate to the U.S. and all of those years they took us on those road trips back to México and instilled in us the importance of family and tradition. My heart was always looking for ways to return to México. The courage that I needed to put in my two-weeks' notice to travel back to the motherland and to have faith that I would be alright came from them, from the example they set going to a country they didn't know, figuring it out, and realizing that it turned out alright for them. I didn't need to find the courage out on an adventure, but the adventure did help me realize that I had courage in me all along as an inheritance from my family. All I needed was to reconnect with it.

❧ 3 ❧

OJOS QUE NO VEN, CORAZÓN
QUE NO SIENTE

"Probablemente ya, de mi te has olvidado
Y mientras tanto yo, Te seguiré esperando
No me he querido ir, Para ver si algún día
Que tu quieras volver, Me encuentres todavía"

— Juan Gabriel, *Se Me Olvidó Otra Vez*

I was standing at the edge of a cliff looking out into the horizon, admiring the beauty of the California sunset, the orange and pink hues covering the sky and the ocean breeze blowing in my hair. The sight was beautiful, and it brought me to tears. This wasn't the first time I had seen a California sunset, but it was the first time I had seen it through different eyes. I had just returned from México after spending two months there. I was back for three weeks, a small break from my México adventure for Thanksgiving and a wedding, and even though I knew I was going back to México in a few weeks, I couldn't help but miss it.

I stood at the edge of the cliff, and I thought of the beauty of this sight, the waves hitting the rocks below the cliff, the birds flying in the sky, and the sun slowly fading away but still glowing on my skin. I thought of how beautiful it was and how I wanted to share it. I was lucky to be standing here, I was lucky to have stood like this at the edge of the ocean in many places around the world to admire the vastness of the world we lived in. I thought of my cousins and friends out in México who would probably never be able to experience this; they would not be able to stand next to me and admire the California sunset overlooking the coast because of man-made borders keeping them away. In that moment, I missed all my friends in México, and I wished one day they would be able to see this beautiful sight in person. That's when I understood it in my heart and acknowledged the privilege of being able to go back and forth from this country to the motherland.

For me, it was as easy as hopping on a plane; for others, the road to the U.S. was much harder. But I must admit, despite my easy access, the emotion of leaving the motherland was one that I was not prepared for. On my flight to L.A. I cried because I knew I would miss everything about México, and the plane held a group of people who probably felt the same way. Grandparents, parents, kids, all going back to the grind in the U.S. and leaving their motherland behind, the place that keeps them connected to family and the place that always feels like home. I cried because México embraced me and welcomed me home, and that is a feeling I've never had from the U.S., being openly embraced and welcomed. That November afternoon, I had gone out for a run in Palos Verdes where there were trails overlooking the ocean and the California rocky coast. I was there because I needed a sanctuary from the hustle and bustle of the city. I needed to reconnect with the tranquil life I had left behind in México, and what better place than in nature?

In the same way that I wanted to share the sights of California with my friends in México, I also wanted to share the beautiful sights of México with those here in the U.S. In México, I would be driving through the green *cerros* of Michoacán and admiring the greenery and the lakes at every turn or hiking up a hill overlooking the rancho— the fields of farmland and the blankets of color in the distance as flowers bloomed all around. I was grateful to be surrounded by such beauty, and I wanted to share that as well. I thought of my family who had become so distant from this place we would visit so often when we were kids, all of my cousins who had not visited in decades, but I also thought of all of the undocumented individuals who, as much as they wanted, would not be able to visit their motherland and the family they left behind because of their legal status. What was this little blue booklet that gave me the right to move around so freely between these two countries? This little blue booklet, this American passport, was privilege.

Privilege comes with great responsibility; in this case, it meant getting to experience things firsthand when most people can't. We have the privilege of seeing places most of our family never thought possible. I think of the moments I spent with my friends in México and how they would come to my *abuela's* house just to hang out. Without internet, one of our forms of entertainment was looking through all my pictures on my computer as if it was a modernized version of a photo album. I appreciated these moments because I couldn't remember the last time I had sat with someone and reminisced through pictures? Sharing my pictures gave them a chance to explore Spain, Paris, London, Morocco, Puerto Rico, and many other places with me as I sat there and shared stories of my adventures. This was also the time where they noticed all the details of the photos that I had never paid attention to, like zooming in on the guys in the background and having a conversation on how hot they were—

and I thought I was detail-oriented! They were eager to hear stories and see people and learn from my experiences, and I was more than willing to share my privilege with them.

In the same way, I came back from México with that same eagerness to share stories of the people, the food, the experiences with anyone who wanted to know more. We often think that many countries can learn a thing or two from the U.S., but similarly, the U.S. can learn a thing or two from other countries— including México. For this to happen, I first needed to be in México in person to experience everything first hand. I needed to be there in person to taste how flavorful the food was and to notice the distinct differences from Mexican food in America and Mexican food in México. I needed to be there in person to experience and receive the warmth and kindness of people in México to recognize how much of my own history was tied to this place, and to appreciate the beauty that surrounded me.

I often tried to hold on to my culture as much as I could in the U.S. because that's what made me unique. I have always been one to be prideful of my Mexican culture, sometimes obnoxiously so. I was that person in college driving down Telegraph Ave. blasting *corridos* just so people would know there was a Mexican at Berkeley because there were so few of us. Music was one of the many ways I held on to my culture, and whenever the mood struck I would always listen to it loudly.

I remember a moment a few years after college. I was getting out of my car at the grocery store in Rancho Cucamonga, a mostly white suburb in California, when a white man asked me, "Do you really listen to that?"

I said, "Yeaaah," annoyed at his question.

I was listening to *tamborazo* on full blast because I was in the mood to dance to the sound of the tuba, the trumpet, and the drums. This music kept me connected to México, to my *rancho*. In any way I could, I tried to learn more about my culture and history. Like many first-generation students in college, I took a Chicano history class to have a deeper understanding of my ethnic history. I would even take the time to explain to friends who some of our cultural icons are, like Vicente Fernandez, the Frank Sinatra of México.

As much as we try to be prideful in our culture, we must acknowledge that we lose a lot of our culture just by being in the U.S. We often rely on what our parents taught us, but we have to be honest and acknowledge that just as much as we have disconnected from the motherland, so have they. Our parents might not be as assimilated to the U.S. as we are, they might speak broken English, they might even eat *frijoles* every day, but they are assimilated to the American lifestyle as much as we were raised in it. I only noticed this going back and paying attention to my dad and some of my tías who were there when I visited. They too have grown accustomed to the luxuries of an American life, and although we rely on them to be our connection to the motherland because they were born there, there is also a disconnect because of the time they have spent in the states. At this point, both of my parents have spent more time living in the states than they spent living in México. Being their kids and identifying as children of immigrants, we use that identity as our connection to the motherland. But at this point, when our parents are on the same boat of assimilation as we are, it now becomes our responsibility, the responsibility of the next generation, to steer the boat back for a visit. If we want to stay connected, we can't solely rely on our parents; we must rely on ourselves.

When I went to México, I decided that I was there to learn, to observe, and to fully immerse myself in the experience. I had to, in order to get the full experience and make the most of my time there. I had to be comfortable with the uncomfortable, open to anything I would have been closed off to before, because if I wasn't, it would be a missed opportunity to learn. I learned to be open to becoming friends with teenagers because they were the last single people in the *rancho*. I learned to live without cell service. I learned to not get annoyed by the flies constantly flying in the kitchen. I learned not to be squeamish when buying meat from the butcher. I learned to squat on toilets I would have never thought I'd have the urgency to use. In the same way, I learned to be thankful and loving. I learned about the *cariño* that everyone carries in their being, and I learned to carry that myself. I learned to be thankful for my immune system while eating questionable food and realizing that our bodies aren't as fragile as we are led to believe. I began to be thankful for the amazing taste of the food because you've never had an authentic Mexican dish until you try it in México with farm fresh ingredients grown in the motherland. I also learned to cook, from scratch!

Ojos que no ven, corazón que no siente— which loosely translated means out of sight, out of mind. But translated in its entirety means eyes that don't see, heart that doesn't feel. We often must see things for ourselves to keep an active thought and feeling about it. With so many years of not visiting México, I had lost sight and connection to this beautiful country. My willingness to see my culture firsthand and to accept it as it is and to learn from it opened my eyes to understanding myself fully. I had the opportunity to hear my family history, understand my family's dynamics, and appreciate the trajectory our family has taken across generations. Some of the most special moments I experienced were those where I sat at the dinner table and listened to my *abuelos* speak for hours at a time. That experience alone fills my heart and brings me to tears because I gave myself the opportunity to do that by going on this adventure. In those moments I thought to myself, no job and no amount of money would be equivalent in value to those moments I shared with my *abuelos*— those moments were priceless.

Similarly, I think of the times I spent with my friends in México, friendships so simple and easy where we would bond sitting out in front of our houses watching cars go by or making a bonfire and cracking jokes so funny that you would almost die of laughter— the kind where you couldn't breath and you got an ab work out as you kept the laughter going. I'm grateful for these friendships because before when I would come to México, I would only be introduced to my parents' friends and relatives who I would often forget about when we went back to California. Now I had my own lifelong friends, who I can visit often or for years to come. I have my own personal connection to the motherland, and it's not just the one my parents left behind.

I hold so much of my motherland in my heart, and I understand the responsibility of being able to share what I know with those that haven't had the opportunity or the privilege to go back and explore in the same way. I can now openly share and pass down the history my *abuelos* shared with me. I can now cook the *pozole* during Christmas and pass down the recipes and the tips and tricks that I learned from my abuela, and I have now made connections in México of my own that will forever keep me tied to this amazing country. I am prepared in so many ways to be a great ancestor for the next generation, to truly hold on to my culture and teach it to the next generation but to also reconnect my parents to it. I see that same disconnect in my parents that I saw in myself when I was trying to figure out what was missing in my life, and I see it fade away when I see them return to their México. Being in the motherland is truly a homecoming that we never knew we were missing, and it is amazing seeing how it fills our hearts.

❧ 4 ❧

NI DE AQUÍ, NI DE ALLÁ

*"We gotta be twice as perfect as anybody else.
We gotta prove to the Mexicans how Mexican we are.
We gotta prove to the Americans how American we are. It's
exhausting! Nobody knows how tough it is to be Mexican-American"*

— Edward James Olmos, in Selena

I used to be the person who had a hard time with labels. I have always been a traveler, and I very much consider myself a global citizen and prefer to be identified as human over any other label separating me into a subgroup. But if push comes to shove, the label that I appreciate most is, *Mexicana*— pronounced in Spanish. I never considered myself fully American because I knew I was Mexican. Additionally, I always took issue with the label of American because, from my experience as a Mexican, I have never been embraced by the U.S. despite it being a country with a mix of cultures and ethnicities. I have always been considered a second-class citizen because of my ethnic background and the color of my skin. I always stood by the idea that I would never use the label of American until this country evolved to one where I would have pride in having that label attached to my identity. As I traveled to Europe when I studied abroad in college, I always identified as Mexican; the only thing close to American I would identify as was Californian.

The reason I love hearing *Mexicana* was because that is what my *señora*, my host mom in Madrid, endearingly called me, "*Mi Mexicana*." This is also what one of my friends who is Puerto Rican has called me, and this is how I describe myself when I am out with one of my group of friends— all of whom are Latinas but among them I am usually the only Mexicana. I love saying it in Spanish too because I am a very strong believer in pronouncing words in the way they are meant to be pronounced, in their native tongue— it sounds so beautiful that way. Living in the states, it can sometimes be difficult to hold on to the correct pronunciation, and I find myself saying things in Spanglish and sometimes with a *gringo* accent. First word that comes to mind is tamale, pronounced *tamal*.

That is the thing about being the first-generation of American born children. We grow up speaking two languages, we're raised in two differing cultures, we navigate two differing value systems, and we can't find where we fit in or where we're meant to be. What's frustrating about the whole experience is that it seems that there is no clear bridge on how to navigate between these two opposing worlds, and it seems like we spend the majority of our time being lost between them.

After having spent time in México, I became more open to my identity as an American. Being in México gave me the opportunity to take ownership of my privilege. That word privilege was something I had always identified with white America. My journey in academia and my professional career always came with the identity of disadvantaged because of all the obstacles I overcame to get to my level of success, given my ethnic background and the neighborhood I grew up in. México turned the tables for me. I remember watching a show on Netflix when I was in México, and it showed a clip of a Richard Pryor comedy special. He was talking about what it felt like as an African-American man to visit the motherland. He said, "It is such a nice feeling because now I know what white people feel in America— relaxed! Because when I heard the police car, I knew they weren't coming after me!"

After I saw that clip I paused the show, and I had a huge epiphany. This was exactly the way I felt being in México. I felt relaxed! It was like a burden was lifted and I no longer had to carry the burden of being a minority anymore. People no longer kept their eyes on me when I entered a store. I no longer felt that comments were racially charged. For the first time, it felt like I was more or less a part of the majority because everyone looked like me.

At the same time, it was also the first time I experienced privilege in the same way that white Americans have. That was hard to wrap my mind around because I had to not only be aware of it but accept it. I had the privilege of living in America, pursuing a college education, making American money, knowing American people, traveling in America and around the world, the privilege of reading, writing, and speaking English! This was the first time I had experienced the privilege I carried in such an intentional way. Mind you, I have always traveled to México and recognized the disparity of wealth and the privilege I had, but those experiences were short-term, a weekend trip to Tijuana or a short week in the rancho. This time, I was living there long-term, building relationships and sharing personal stories that would highlight the privilege that I carried. For the first time in my life, I fully identified with the word privileged.

Being in those long-term relational experiences did not give me the ability to ignore or hide behind the discomfort of feeling my privilege around those who did not have it. What I appreciated in those moments was having had my own personal experience of being disadvantaged in America. It's so bizarre to think that I would actually appreciate those experiences, but they helped me practice humility, especially in a place like the *rancho* where humility is one of the most beautiful qualities of the people. I had been on both sides of the spectrum: in America I'm disadvantaged, and in México I'm privileged. My ability to identify with both is what ultimately helped me navigate the way I carried my privilege when I was in México.

It's funny because walking around in America, I have *"el nopal en la frente"*— a saying that is often used by Mexicans to articulate that by looks alone you look hella Mexican. In the same way, walking around in México, people from the ranchos could straight up tell I was from *"El Norte."* Despite toning down everything, wearing jeans and a basic t-shirt, *huaraches*, no jewelry, and hardly any make-up, people could still tell I was from the U.S. Some of these experiences gave me a good laugh. One time my cousins and I were waiting for the bus in front of a church. I was walking around, and I passed by the *paletero* selling ice cream from his cart. He literally said, "Ice cream, ice cream." I responded back in Spanish jokingly telling him that I didn't want any right now. I went back and told my cousins about it, and we laughed at the fact that even though I was wearing my *huaraches* and my Mexican embroidered shirt, this man could tell I was American and used the English he knew to try to sell me an ice cream. The hustle was real! And I appreciated it.

There was another time when we were walking in Quiroga, the town in Michoacán where *carnitas* originated from; you have dozens of men selling tacos and giving you a sample of the savory slow-cooked pork as you pass by. It's like walking around Costco for samples, only better because these are mouthwatering homemade *carnitas*. As we were walking, one of these men said, "Welcome! Where are you from?". My cousin who was walking in front said in her most American voice, "California?" confused and with a little laughter in her voice wondering why this man spoke to her in English. After the whole ordeal, my cousin and I laughed about it because people can straight up tell we're not from there, but we understand they speak to us in English for kicks and probably to practice with us.

I also had moments when my Spanish brought a bit of laughter because I used the wrong word or pronounced it differently. One day, I was buying bread from my cousin's best friend who would drive through the *pueblos* and sell *pan dulce* from her truck. I asked for a *trompazo* rather than a *trompada* — I basically asked her to punch me in the face instead of the sweet, pig-shaped *pan dulce* that I like. It's hard to keep up with because Spanish words change from region to region, but the reason I did so well was because of my curiosity in asking "What does that mean?" when I didn't know a specific word.

It is moments like these that made me realize how much I will never fully fit into the identity of Mexican despite how much I tried. The one difference I must point out is that despite being from *El Norte*, I was still embraced fully and appreciated in México. Those moments where people pointed out my Americanness were never hateful; they might have been with a joking undertone, but more often than not, I was approached with curiosity and understanding. Whereas whenever my identity has been pointed out in America, more often than not, it has been with a negative racial bias.

With all these varying experiences in México and new perspectives I had gained, especially those around my identity, I was finally able to identify with being American, in my own way. Before, my idea of American was the privilege white America held and the visuals of Americans in mainstream media. Even with the efforts of diversity, America has rarely represented my family's story of immigration. The visual of the American Dream I had always been presented with was having a corporate career, a house, a family, and a white picket fence, and for whatever reason, I never identified with that dream. The moment that I realized my American Dream was when I found a new way to identify with my American identity. This happened in a conversation with my dear friend Mariana, who at nineteen years old— ten years younger than me— was my best friend in the *rancho*. In America, I find myself spending hours in conversations with friends analyzing and articulating complicated concepts of our identities and the problems of the world. My conversations with Mariana were different; the conversations with all my friends in México were simple. There was nothing complicated about them, and that is what I loved. There was no analyzing, no judgement, it was mostly storytelling and getting to know each other by sharing what we liked.

Mariana and I were sitting outside of my *abuelas* house on a bench talking about TV shows we liked to watch. It was so nice to almost teleport myself back into my teenage years through these conversations that brought back the feeling of hanging out with my high school friends, flipping through magazines and just having a fun time being around each other. We spent a good while talking about movies and just retelling the plot lines, it was as simple as that. We got to the place where we realized we both loved watching Grey's Anatomy. At one point, I was trying to remember one of the character's names, and I was describing him— the good-looking doctor with the colored eyes, he's African-American, and he's the plastic surgeon— and she remembered the name,

Dr. Avery! After discussing the show for a few more minutes and sharing how the last season ended, she told me how she wished she could meet a black person one day, because she loved all the characters in Grey's Anatomy. It had never occurred to me, until that moment, that she was not exposed to the diverse cultures that I have been. But, duh, this was rural México. The only places I saw non-Mexicans in México were in the cities, and even then, they were rare. In that moment, I understood even more of the privilege of being American. I had exposure to the many diverse cultures around the world because of the melting pot that America is. I personally had a diverse group of friends, I've had the opportunities to learn about their cultures, and I've had the opportunity to try different ethnic foods.

This was the moment that my identity as an American shifted. Being American for me was no longer about the American Dream and the white picket fence and how unaligned my ideals were from it. Being American was now my own experience of diversity, of being lucky enough to meet people different than me and to explore their cultures by what they shared with our country. For the first time, I identified with the label of American because I was now able to share my experiences in the U.S. with those who did not have the privilege of experiencing them in México.

When I came back to México after attending my friend's wedding in California, I made sure to share the pictures of the wedding with my friends Mariana and Estrella. The wedding was a Chinese/Vietnamese wedding with a traditional tea ceremony. They were in love with the pictures, and they asked about the traditions. I was excited to tell them about it and be able to describe things in terms related to our culture. Though both cultures were very different, there were a lot of aspects that were very much the same. They had a roasted pig, and I told them it tasted like *carnitas*, something from our culture in Michoacán that they could identify with. I also shared how my friend had an uncle who reminded me of one of ours and how they also lit fireworks after the ceremony, which was similar to us lighting fireworks for any of our celebrations, and they had an undeniable reverence for their elders like we did in México. Being American for me in this moment was the bridging of cultures in two parts of the world with two sets of people that I loved.

I used to have the feeling of tug-of-war with two opposing cultures and values, not knowing which way to go. It was almost as if these two cultures were on separate islands; I had to go back and forth on a small paddle boat and figure out where I liked spending most of my time. It was exhausting! Now I feel that with everything that I've learned and my new perspective, I've built a bridge across these two islands, and I walk freely between both with plenty to share when I come for a visit. I'm like the perfect guest in these two islands because I come baring gifts and stories to share. As a matter of fact, I've created my own space, a tree-house if you will, on this bridge because this is where I feel like I most belong. I am the bridging of two cultures, openly experiencing and openly teaching both cultures to others. What I hadn't realized about my identity before was that I had to take a deeper dive into it in order to fully understand and articulate my experience with both of my identities.

This became even more clear when I was traveling solo and made a few international friends from Spain, Peru, and México. When I studied abroad back in college, it was easy for me to be Mexicana because out in Spain there were not too many other Mexicans to compare me to. However, in México you could tell the difference between someone born and raised there and myself with my American mannerisms. What was interesting in those moments was explaining my experience of being considered an ethnic minority in the U.S.

This came about when talking about the political climate and discussing the influence of racism in the U.S. This may have been the first time or one of the few times my new friends had a discussion with someone with a dual cultural identity who has experienced racial bias in the country they were born in. This was also eye-opening for me because I realized avid travelers, people who actively go seeking and learning about other people's culture, often only get exposed to the ethnic majority in the countries they visit, which made expressing my dual-identity that much more important.

When people travel the world they go to experience the culture of the country, that often doesn't include the culture of people with dual-identities. This made me realize that not too many people around the world can identify with two distinct cultures, and although it can often be a burden, it can also be a blessing in moments like this when I can openly talk about my experience and possibly open the eyes of those who might never have encountered it before.

When I first arrived in México, it was as if I had heart-shaped eyes as soon as I walked out of the plane. On the drive to Michoacán from Guadalajara, I admired all the fields of agave and the amazing tequila that it would become. I admired the greenery and the rain as we drove by hills and nature surrounding all the small towns. I admired all the men and women sitting outside of their homes people watching and paying attention to the cars that drove by. This admiration of my motherland kept my eyes so open that I could no longer ignore what I should be admiring about the U.S. With this I was able to acknowledged one of my favorite privileges in the U.S. was the ability to know people from different walks of life. One of the perks of that was also being able to choose what kind of food I wanted to eat that day— Thai, Indian, Korean, Salvadorian, Mexican, Japanese, Mediterranean— and my ability to know people tied to these cultures and delicious dishes. It was my ability to see similarities in families so culturally different than my own but to understand that in many ways we were just the same. We all tend to have that funny uncle, the elegant aunt, the stoic cousin, and the baby that everyone loves.

With that said, there is still a big part of the American identity that I struggle with. That is the racial disparity of our country. I can acknowledge and accept my identity and the privilege that comes with being American, but I can never stand and be fully proud of it. Not until my Mexican side is seen as equally important as my American side, and not until every minority is treated equally as American as well. Part of the work then becomes being a part of the process that pushes the country to evolve into a one that strives to treat everyone equally. For that I will always say I'm Mexican-American or Mexicana and hold true to the roots of where I come from. There's still a lot of work to be done in the U.S. and that is the main reason I returned. My hope is to help bridge the divide and racial disparity in the U.S. by connecting others with their ancestral wisdom passed down from our parents and elders by recognizing that we are worth it! By recognizing that other people fought and survived to be here because they thought we were worthy of it. Sometimes we have to go on an exploratory journey to recognize how true that is. México provided that for me.

I've always been an admirer of other cultures, and I have always been proud of mine. But this time, I went into this experience as if I was studying abroad. With that open-mindedness, I was able to learn and admire my own Mexican culture through travelers' eyes that made me appreciate it even more. In the same way, I was able to view the U.S. with those travelers' eyes when I returned as I enjoyed the diversity that a city like Los Angeles has to offer. Understanding that both countries have much to offer its people brought me a sense of humility because I now understood that I was lucky enough to experience both. Not to say that I overlooked the flaws that both countries have, but for the first time I was able to acknowledge that both of my identities carried something special and being able to recognize that and express it and share it with others was what made me special. *Ni de aquí, ni de allá*— not from here, nor from there, but from everywhere.

5

NO ME SE RAJAR

"A mi no me asustan tipos lengua larga
Que solo presumen para apantallar
Yo soy de los hombres que no temen nada
Y aunque este perdido no me se rajar"

— José Carmen Frayle Castañón, *No Se Me Se Rajar*

I grew up knowing that my parents left their motherland to provide a better life for our family. I've listened to countless stories of people's journeys through the border on the news, in movies, and even from my own family. My brother and I once volunteered with an organization in San Diego, called Border Angels, whose humanitarian efforts organize groups of volunteers to bring gallons of water out into the desert as a lifeline for people who go on the treacherous journey. On that Saturday morning, almost a hundred people showed up with two gallons of water each and a pack of survival essentials. We hiked for a few miles in the California desert, scattering gallons of water and the bags of supplies we had brought with us all around the desert in hopes that these supplies would be a life-line to someone who needed it. It was February, but even then it was still hot, and the gallons we were carrying were heavy; I was sweating and a little dehydrated, and after a couple of miles I knew I wasn't wearing the proper shoes.

Despite all of that, I was grateful that I was only going on this short journey to help and not because this journey was required of me to pursue a better life. I thought of the moms who have made this journey with their young children in their arms, who weigh as much if not more than the two gallons of water in my hands, and that was enough to keep me going. I thought about my shoes and how I was going to be able to change out of them soon. Most people who made this journey cross with nothing, so I was lucky to go back to my regular life after this. I was grateful that my parents had gone on this journey for me. They had made the sacrifice so I wouldn't have to.

The next morning, we had a family breakfast, and my brother and I shared the experience with my parents. First, my mom asked why we didn't invite her. Second, this conversation opened the door for our parents to share their experience crossing the border.

My dad had crossed the desert in the same way, only with a group of men and in the middle of the night to avoid being conspicuous. He described it being so dark that they often didn't know what they were stepping on. The journey was so long and tiring that one of the men in his group was just about ready to give up. This man was struggling keeping up with their pace and continuing forward and had said he was turning around and to go back to México.

The man said, "*Ya no puedo, mejor me regreso.*"

My dad then said, "*Como que te vas a regresar, lo que vas a caminar pa' México lo puedes caminar pa' delante;*" he told this man to think about his kids because they were already halfway there and too keep moving forward.

Walking back to México would have been the same distance if he continued forward, so they kept going and made it through. My dad came when he was young, and I can picture him in his youth from the picture my grandma has of him hanging on her wall. Even then, he was the man I know now, the leader that he has always been, always getting people to see what they are capable of.

That wasn't the only time he had to cross the border illegally. When he and my mom got married they decided to make their life out here in the U.S., he had to cross over illegally again because he wasn't going to let her cross on her own. They crossed the border again and were caught and detained. I had never heard this story before, and I realized there is so much our parents don't tell us of their suffering because they don't want us to ever experience it ourselves. But we have to hear these stories because they serve as a reminder of where our courage, strength and desire for a better life comes from. My parents tried again, and this time they crossed hidden in between merchandise of an eighteen-wheeler truck with a group of people standing so tightly together in a dark and closed off space that it was difficult for them to breathe. But they made it.

I think about this and the countless stories of immigration that I've heard from friends, and I can't help but feel immense pride in these people that, despite the odds, are still here giving it their all in the U.S. With that, I'm sure you can imagine my hesitation in telling my parents that I was planning to live in México for a few months. After their journey to get here, I didn't want to disrespect their sacrifice and I was hesitant in telling them I was planning to go back and live in México. But I had to let them know.

We were driving back home from Sunday night dinner

one evening in April, my lease was up that month and my parents were asking what I was going to do about it. I told my parents that I was not planning on renewing the lease.

They asked, "Then where are you going to live?"

Hopeful that I would say I'd be moving back in with them. I hesitated for a second and thought to myself it's now or never.

I casually said "México."

My mom replied, "*¿Que?! Como que te vas pa' México. Nosotros que nos fuimos de allá y tu que te quieres regresar.*"

She was appalled that I wanted to go live in México confused as to why I would want to live in the country they had left.

In that moment, I don't think they believed I was being serious. But with all the crazy adventures I had been on in the past they at least knew to humor me with more questions. They asked where I was going to stay and I said in the *rancho* with my *abuelos*.

My dad said "*Pues que bien.*"

In that moment he was on board because that meant I would be around to help out his parents. I found this surprising because I thought they both would be opposed.

I think my mom thought it was one of my crazy ideas. After this conversation they didn't bring it up again. The thing about me and my crazy ideas is that I always make them come to fruition, so when I left my apartment and moved in for a couple of weeks, even after I put in my two weeks' notice and up until I was getting dropped off at the airport, my parents didn't believe I was actually going through with this.

As my mom dropped my dad and I off at the airport she asked with teary eyes "*De verdad te vas a quedar en México?*"

I said yes and we hugged and she gave me her *bendición* with the sign of the cross and a kiss and she drove away.

This journey was something that was in my heart, and I somehow was brave enough to go through with it, brave enough to leave my job, and brave enough to have faith that I could survive on my savings and faith that this journey would be worthwhile.

Granted, not everyone can make the same drastic move in their life and go full *Eat, Pray, Love* to México, but for me it was possible; I had nothing holding me back but myself. From the moment I decided to go on this journey and as the months passed by, I became more and more committed to the idea, and I began to fall in love with my sense of adventure that had been lost for some time now. I began to play around with the endless possibilities of this path. Could I teach English while I was there? Could I get a job at an international company in México? Could I start my own business out there? The idea that I no longer had to be tied to the American Dream in the U.S. was so liberating because I recognized that anything could be possible.

Strangely enough, I began associating this freedom of dreaming about possibilities to what my parents must have gone through when they dreamed about coming to America. They grew up poor in a rural town México with huge families were there was barely enough to go around, and everyone had to work to earn their keep and make ends meet. The idea of coming to America must have been so grand for them. I reflect back on it now, and I know there were at least three things my parents would have needed to make that journey across the border— courage, strength, and faith: courage to take the first step and leave everything they knew behind them and to step into the unknown; strength to physically and emotionally go through the journey itself; and faith that there would be something better on the other side of the border. For them, this was all true. They had the courage to go on the journey, the strength to make it through, and with their faith, they made their American Dream come true.

When I graduated college, I thought that graduating and having that college degree hanging in my parent's living room was their American Dream, and to an extent, it was. But being in México and hearing stories about my parents' lives when they were younger made me realize that their dream, the dream when they were my age, was to raise a family in America. That was it! My parents made their own dream come true, regardless of whether or not I had that college degree. Everything their kids accomplished was just the cherry on top or the frosting. But the cake, was them making their life in America, buying a house and having a family. That realization took the pressure off.

Completely disconnecting and letting go of the idea that I had to make my parents' American Dream come true was so liberating. For the first time ever, I gave myself permission to make my own dream. For me, my dream has always been traveling outside of the U.S. My heart was pulling me to México. For the first time ever, I followed the example of my parents and made my dream come true in another country. I've always tried to make my parents proud— and I know I have with all my accomplishments— but there always comes a time where you have to fly out of the nest for yourself.

For me, that was flying back to México despite my parents' opposition. They were worried about my safety. Which made me imagine the opposition my grandma might have had when my dad left for the U.S. when he was only fourteen, she mentioned it from time to time when I was in México, which made me recognize that she still felt that. As children, we're always going to do something that our parents will not agree with but when we do those things, we must do them knowing they are for our best interest. When I shared what I wanted to do with my life, and what that looked like for me, though hesitant at the beginning, my parents started to be strangely supportive, maybe because they themselves related to this idea of going on a journey for a better life.

My parents crossed the border north to provide for their family and for financial survival. They believed a better life constituted of education and better economic opportunities. Now that I've had the privilege of having received the benefits of stability, my belief is that a better life means seeking fulfillment. Fulfillment for me was finding peace between the conflict of my opposing identities, and I was able to find that in this journey. When I found peace, I also found cultural wisdom and traditions that I could pass down to the next generation. It's difficult to think about it, but when our parents pass, who's going to keep those traditions alive? Who's going to cook the *pozole* and make the *tamales* for Christmas? I was raised with *pozole* made from scratch; there's no way I can have the same satisfaction with pozole from a can. The thought of my niece and nephews not appreciating *pozole* like my siblings and I do breaks my heart, so who else is going to cook it but me?

This is why buying that flight to México was so important. I bought it without asking for approval from anyone but with enough time to prepare myself and others of my journey. It forced me to have those difficult conversations with family of the reasons why I was doing it. It forced us to reflect on what it meant reconnecting to the motherland. It also forced me to practice voicing exactly what I wanted. For the longest time, I was always the provider, the one who took care of everything and everyone. For the first time ever, I put myself first. The more and more I told friends, family, and colleagues about my planned adventure, the more real it became and the less space *para rajarme, porque no me se rajar*. Backing out was not an option.

I went forward with the steps to prepare, such as saving as

much as I could in the months before my trip. I did as much research as I could. This included watching documentaries on the cartels in Michoacán. I wanted to make sure I knew what I could because I was walking into a state in México that has a *Level 4: Do Not Travel* advisory by the U.S. Department of State. I looked at crime maps, blogs, videos online, and to be honest, I was psyching myself out and back-pedaling on my decision. What if I get kidnapped?

During this time of preparation, I had a trip planned to Tijuana to donate several bags of stuff from when I moved out of my apartment. We met a young woman named Ana, a twenty-six-year-old mother of two from none other than Michoacán. She was at a women's shelter because she was on her journey seeking asylum in México. She was scared for her children's lives and her own; their home and store had been robbed by people she thought might have been part of a cartel collecting quotas from small business owners. I thought this was a sign from the universe that I shouldn't go, but even then I still wanted to. Despite the real fear of danger from Ana's story, I still needed to go. I thought maybe I would go and see how things are and then come back in a month. In that moment of hearing Ana's story, I recognized she had no other choice than to seek asylum. I, on the other hand, was privileged enough not to be in her situation. I had family in México but most importantly men in my life, who in México are still seen as a sign of family protection. She had neither; the only family she had was her mom. Everyone else was on the other side of the border. I had family on both sides of the border, and luckily enough, my family was on the east side of Michoacán, which doesn't have too much violent crime.

With all this research and reflection on my pre-journey, I really began to doubt my decision. I remember driving home still feeling some type of way when I received a notification that I had gotten a financial gift from a friend. I called her immediately and asked why. I expressed my gratitude, especially in that moment when I needed to be grounded, and my concerns about my safety and traveling in México. She said something that resonated with me, and I held onto it the entire time I was in México. I had known this before when I studied abroad in Europe, and now I was being reminded of it again.

She said, "No matter where you go, there's going to be bad things happening everywhere, but there are always going to be good people everywhere too."

She was right. In that moment, I thought of all the people I encountered in my travels whose kindness I had to rely on, and there were numerous. The day before my flight, I went in with a renewed energy and the reminder that there are kind people everywhere. This was also the reminder I used and shared with my *abuela* to ease her anxiety when I would go into the city by myself. This was the truest thing in México: kindness surrounded me, and I experienced that the entire time I was there, I was grateful *que no me raje*.

✺ 6 ✺

PRIMERO DIOS

"Un día a la vez, Dios mío.
Es lo que pido de ti.
Dame la fuerza para vivir un día a la vez."

— Los Tigres del Norte, *Un Día a la Vez,*

After returning from my adventure in México I went on a weekend a trip to Illinois to visit my other *abuela*. I was sitting at the breakfast table at my *tío's* house eating *chilaquiles* and *carnitas*, and I loved that we were having interesting discussions about life and about México. Both my uncle and I agreed that if we could, we would go out and live life in México because life was so simple and tranquil out there. There was no rush; life just happens as slowly as it does, nothing to stress you out and nothing to worry about. I told him that what I loved about it was that everyone lived by this philosophy of *"Primero Dios"*— God willing. You can be in conversation talking to someone, and before departing, you can tell them, I'll see you tomorrow, and they'll say, *"Primero Dios"* or *"Si Dios Quiere."* When I left México I told my *abuela* that I would be coming back to visit later in the year, and she would say *"Primero Dios."* This idea of leaving it up to God was freeing coming from a place where I would schedule every single minute of the day and then going to México where there were no deadlines, time constraints, or schedules; it was all *"Primero Dios"*— leave it up to God.

This was the first time that I was allowed to live life exactly as it was. I was just me. I was not the college graduate, the working professional, the daughter of immigrants. I was just me, the simplest version of myself. No labels, no expectations. It helped that no one really cared about the jobs I had held in the past or even the academic accomplishments I came with. I just left all of that at the border. My conversations were not about work or career or education. Instead, I had conversations about my family, about my travels, about my interests, about all the things that made me uniquely me. Most importantly, this space of liberation gave me a place to listen to others and a place to be present in the now.

I had no schedule, so I didn't have to worry about what I was doing tomorrow or the day after. The most I had to worry about was if I had to go into town to get el *mandado*— food we needed or anything else we needed for the house. For the first time ever, I was living by the sun. I woke up as the sunlight filled my room. I would cook and clean and be of service to my *abuelos*. No matter where I was in the day, my body could tell what time it was. If it was about to be 3:00 p.m., I would start to feel hungry and knew it was time to go home. If it was after sunset, my body could tell at what time I should go to bed. Every morning I would wake up at exactly the same time, 7:51 a.m., exactly after eight hours of sleep. This was the first time that I noticed the positioning of the sun and how it would change with the seasons. I felt in tune with life and connected to the world because of the sun. I couldn't remember the last time I had paid that much attention to nature. Working in an office the majority of the day, there were plenty of times where I wouldn't even see natural sunlight.

Being so present in those moments let me be in a place of gratitude. My morning meditations allowed me to be present in that exact moment, to notice the pink *colchas* on the bed I was sitting on, the bright peach color of the walls in the room, the brightness of the sunlight coming through the windows in the morning, the black-and-white portrait of my *abuelo* when he was young and holding his first born, the portrait of my *bisabuelo* showing the age and life on his face through his wrinkles and stern look. I could acknowledge that I was in that room, that there was nature all around me surrounding the house and that farther out of México was my family in California, and then come back to that room where I was sitting and concentrating on my breathing and being appreciative of the space I had given myself living in México. This transformed how I went about my day because I was so grateful to be there in the present. There were so many moments where I would sit at the dinner table in silence with my *abuelos*, and I was just happy to be there sharing a meal with them, observing how my *abuelo's* strong hands would shake as he used his spoon to scoop up his food, or how he always made sure my *abuela* had a napkin next to her a simple sign of him caring for her, and how my *abuela* would take her time chewing her food. These small moments of love made me appreciate the example they set for my family.

Being in this place and noticing all the details in those moments didn't come easy. It took about a month into my stay until I finally started to wind down from all the stress I had accumulated over the year. The first two weeks I was there, my dad was there with me; the third week, my *tía*, *tío*, and *prima* were there. It wasn't until they had all gone back to the states that the reality of my decision hit me. I was actually living in México. I freaked out and I remember spending one afternoon spiraling into fear trying to calculate how long my savings would last me. I figured I only needed to be there at the very least until *Día de Los Muertos* which was a month away. If I made it that far then I could just buy a flight back home and start looking for work before my money ran out, that way my unemployment gap wouldn't look so bad on my resume. It took so much work on my part not to let the anxiety I was experiencing take over. I made it a habit to spend the mornings in prayerful meditation, and I would spend some time in the afternoon reading one of the many books I brought with me. It was easy because I had no cell service inside my *abuelos* house, so mindlessly scrolling through my phone in the morning was no longer an issue and picking up a book was easy. The most important part of it all was connecting and spending time with others, whether it was my *abuelos* or my new friends.

My main mantra while living in México was "How can I see this differently?" This especially came in handy when I was doing something that made me uncomfortable. If we had just re-heated food that had been sitting out all night in the counter I would think, "Well this is still the best *caldo* that I've had. It's organic, and we're about to find out how good of an immune system I actually have." If my *abuela* told me to go to my *tía's* and hang out with my *prima*, I would say I was fine staying home and reading or doing something to keep busy. But then I realized being busy and doing something alone was where I was comfortable. Going out there and relating to my teenage cousins and her friends was a different experience because I spent so much of my adult life with adults. I let discomfort be my guide. I was used to planning, scheduling, trying new restaurants and new experiences, texting "Let me know when you're here", and spending a lot of time alone. All of that didn't work in the *"Primero Dios"* culture. I had to go with the flow, drop by to people's houses unannounced, yell people's names through the door and hope they would answer, spend time with friends doing nothing, be okay with plans changing last minute and not be upset about it. It was refreshing, and I understood that if you leave it up to God and have faith, things might end up better than you planned.

I don't know exactly what I was expecting out of México. I think for the most part I was expecting to find peace, stillness, good food, and to get to know my *abuelos*. Not only did I get that, but I got so much more.

What I loved about the rancho was people's humility. People don't have much here; what little money they have they work hard for it, and what they own in material possessions they take care of. Money isn't flaunted as it is in the states, and when it's received, it is appreciated. Another phrase that I heard constantly was *"Que Dios te lo pague"*— may God repay you. Any time money was given to someone or a kind gesture was given, people would say *"Que Dios te lo pague"* because they themselves had nothing to give. Here in the states, it is so hard to give a gift because people often think of how they are going to reciprocate; it's sometimes difficult to do a favor for someone because people often feel indebted since popular culture in the U.S. is "you scratch my back, I scratch yours." When people say, "May God repay you" it takes it out of your hands and leaves it up to God to repay a good deed. The humility of people in México helped me to fully grasp this concept and bring it with me to the states. This thought allowed me to not only give freely, but also receive freely. Before México I would often say, "It's okay you don't have to do that," when anyone offered their help, I thought I was just being polite and at the same time fiercely independent. I have now changed to accepting and receiving kindness by saying "Thank you, I'd love your help!" and understanding that help is a gift from people and I shouldn't prevent their generosity and that one day if I can repay them I will, but also God will continue to bless them in many ways.

This whole idea of God so intertwined in the daily lives of people in México really got me thinking. For the most part, I've grown up in America where the freedom of religion is an inalienable right. How beautiful is it to be in a place that grants freedom to believe what you want and there's a diversity in spiritual thought, but I think I mistook that as not being able to express my spirituality publicly. I often shied away from speaking of my spirituality for fear of offending someone. Through my curiosity I've come to understand the beauty of a lot of different religions, and I respect that every spiritual practice has an undertone of love and community. When we're so busy telling people why their view of religion and love is wrong, we're blinded by the way people are actually putting love into practice. Having not gone to a Catholic mass since the last time my mom guilted me into it, I recognized I had to reconcile with it because at the very least this was the way I was introduced to God. Once I understood that, it was easy for me to see the positive influence that spirituality had in México. I could not deny that the reason so many Mexican elders were so kind and loving and would share life lessons was because they felt called to share this through their faith in God.

On December 12, el *Día de La Virgen de Guadalupe* I was able to truly see the influence and the history *La Virgen* had in México. I was captivated by a black and white film that was on TV that illustrated the indigenous culture and the conquest from Spain. *La Virgen*, when she appeared to Juan Diego was a way that indigenous people could stay connected to their indigenous culture and accept the new religion that was forced upon them. Because looking back at indigenous cultures, we can't deny that spirituality was a big part of it.

The *virgen* provided a way that they could relate to this new religion. This day was a day of celebration that began with a procession in the pueblo beginning in *la capilla*. These celebrations were a way for the people of México to continue to express their cultural traditions and spirituality in a way that was acceptable for the colonizers. This is why as a country, México has so much reverence for *La Virgen de Guadalupe*.

All the women and the young girls dressed as *guares* and all the boys dressed as Juan Diego. They followed along the two people leading the procession carrying a large portrait of *La Virgen* through the *pueblo*. The elders of the town waited sitting in front of their house and the portrait would be presented to them as the procession approached. I saw how my grandma almost in tears expressed her gratitude to *La Virgen* as she touched the portrait and said a small prayer and my grandpa who isn't a very religious man, still had a reverence for *La Virgen* as he made the sign of the cross and said a small prayer himself. As we moved along the pueblo I also noticed how cars that would pass by would stop as they saw the procession and the men in the car would remove their *tejanas* and make the sign of the cross to pay their respects.

Besides *El Día de La Virgen de Guadalupe*, every pueblo had their own holiday to celebrate *la virgen* or the patron saint. Similar to the story of Juan Diego, these celebrations were also attached to a story of a miracle appearance from a *virgen* and the *fiestas* would be a celebration of that miracle. These religious celebrations have been a place to conserve the indigenous culture that we originate from. These are the days where we go back and dress in our traditional attire and dance through the pueblo in celebration, this is where the new generations get introduced to our cultural traditions. These are the days where we come back and learn more about our roots.

With this new understanding of religion I began to also

understand the lifestyle associated with these beliefs. México helped me understand that I was raised conservatively. Being in the rancho, I realized how conservative people were about dating, gender roles, sexuality, religion, etc. I also realized that was how my parents grew up and how they raised us. I only started being liberal when I went off to college and started learning about politics and social justice. I would be caught off-guard when someone would make a very conservative comment because I was so used to hanging out with very liberal people. In those moments, I tried to understand rather than question or challenge, and that helped me immensely. I was there to learn from the *rancho* and its simplicity in life, not to try to teach and impose my beliefs on them. What also surprised me was that the young adults were very much open-minded about diversity, acceptance, and equality. At one of the high school events, the teenagers had posters representing diversity of all different ethnicities, religions, sexual orientation, and equal rights. Despite their conservative values, people were still very much supportive of personal freedoms. What I realized was that people are multifaceted, people can be conservative and still be supporters of diversity and equal rights. We're all human and learning in the process.

One night I was on the phone with a friend, and she was asking what it was like being in México. I described it as "real country:" most people were married and had kids when they were young, and by these standards, I was considered an old spinster. I was surrounded by farmland and everyone was pretty much a cowboy. I even said, to put it into context, "It's like a small farm town in Mississippi." That's when it hit me; if I was in America, I would literally be in the most conservative part of it. In the midst of it all, I realized that I was a city girl with country values because I was raised by my parents who were raised in the country, but I developed my own liberal values when they migrated to the city. Which reminded me of a conversation I had with my mom where she brought up her concern of how liberal Berkeley was, I didn't understand her question then but I did now.

This made me recognize that with independence comes transformation, and not everyone has that privilege of creating an independent identity. When I came to this realization, that my identity was a transformation of differing ideals, I recognized that, despite some difference in opinions, I was still able to love and care for the people in the *rancho*, who were, for the most part, conservative. Part of that was because I recognized through my experience in México I could now be a bridge of these polarizing political ideals. So I asked myself, would it be that difficult to feel the same way about conservative Americans? It might be more difficult given the political climate, but given this experience, I was now open to try and let go of my judgements and assumptions. I was so in tune with the question "How can I see this differently?" that some realizations would come to me without even asking, just by pure faith that I would get the answer if I just payed attention.

I was so dedicated to being in the moment and paying attention to the details that I kept getting new insights into my life from small and simple conversations. A big shift in my understanding of my family life happened when my *abuela* was telling me about when my dad first went to *El Norte*. She talked about how young he was when he first left, with her eyes looking at her hands as she twiddled her thumbs, almost expressing regret that she couldn't do more to keep him home and be able to provide more. I recognized her sadness, which I had never seen before. But how could you not be sad when most of your family left and are still gone? In that moment I recognized the hurt my *abuelos* experienced when not only my dad, but their daughters also left in search of a better life in the U.S. There was hurt, but also understanding because she knew it was something they had to do to provide a better life for themselves. This brought compassion to not only my *abuelos* but my parents.

When I first went off to college I practically had an argument with my parents wondering why they wouldn't let me go despite all of my hard work. They eventually came around, but there was this underlying resentment I carried because they did not provide the kind of support I wanted, that I had to fight for it despite how much I had already proven myself. In that moment, looking at my *abuela* I realized that my parents not wanting to let me go was maybe less about their concern of me being on my own and being a woman, but more of them not wanting me to experience the pain and hurt of being away from home. Looking back at it now, that first year of college was hard! I can only imagine what that first year in the U.S. was like for my parents, not speaking the language, the culture-shock, the racism. Maybe what they said was that they wanted me close in case of an emergency, but I recognize now that maybe they were just trying to protect me from the pain of being on my own and alone, protect me like any good parent would. And maybe they were also were trying to keep me home, because of the guilt they themselves felt leaving their parents behind in México and the guilt they still feel now. Maybe they were also trying to keep me from carrying my own guilt. Which is why I am now able to look at these memories with so much compassion.

So many conversations like these happened that brought forth new insights. There was another time when my *tío* was sharing how much he hated visiting México City when my *abuela* was in the hospital. I was surprised because from my perspective people loved going to México City. I asked him why and he said people always looked at him funny because he was from the *rancho*. That moment made me pause and

and take into account how often I was judgmental of people in middle America, because of my assumption that they were too country for me to relate to. How often did I have that assumption when thinking of the last presidential election? In that moment I recognized my arrogance, the one that my uncle was speaking of. I was that person in the city who he was talking about, at the end of the day people are people and we need to see them as such. I know that my uncle is intelligent, hard-working and caring and the only thing that separates him from people in the city is opportunity. Would that not be the same for people in middle America?

Another instance when this realization deepened was when I was in México City and I realized that *banda* music was the country music of México. I grew up thinking that everywhere in México people listened to *banda*. That is, until I realized that in other places, especially the cities and beach towns they listen to *salsa*, *merengue*, and *cumbias*. I was that person who listened to all types of music except country, now I recognize that is not completely true because I listen to *banda*, and *banda* and *corridos* are México's country music. These realizations kept happening because I was open to learning from every interaction and conversation and having faith that everything was teaching me something new. Additionally, I was willing to let my curiosity guide me and ask all the "dumb" questions like, everyone doesn't listen to *banda*?

At one point, I was even grateful for all the student loans that I had. This was when I was paying my bills online because, despite having left my job, there were still a lot of expenses I had to take care of. In trying to see my loans differently, I recognized that I needed them in order to go to college away from home. Going to college on my own helped me recognize the courage needed to start anew in a place unknown. Doing that then gave me the courage to study abroad, and that ignited my passion for cultural travel.

Without that passion, would I have left my job to live in México? I don't know for sure, but all that set me up for this journey, and I was so happy and grateful for being here. I was feeling a bit anxious about my savings lasting through my time there, but I realized that support comes in different forms and money was just one of them.

One of the ways I received support was from my *tía*. When she would call, she would tell me not to spend any of my savings on groceries because she had sent money to take care of that for my *abuelos*. It was hard for me, but whenever my *abuela* would insist on giving me money for *el mandado* I would accept it. Most of the time, I would pay for things myself because everything was so cheap, but whenever my *abuela* insisted on giving me money, I would take it because I knew that both my *tía* and my *abuelos* were so grateful that I was there helping around the house and taking care of them that they didn't mind simply paying for food. I also understood that as the elders they also appreciated their roles as providers, and I didn't want to take that away from them. Every time I would head into town, my *abuelo* would get up and search through his pockets for money to buy him something that he needed; this reminded me so much of when I was a kid and they would slip us money folded in their hand and say "*Para que te compres una paleta*". I even saw them do this to my eight-year-old niece, and I understood that no matter how old I am, I will always be their granddaughter. The hardest one to receive was the day that I left and my abuela tried to slip me five hundred pesos, equivalent to about twenty dollars. She said "*Para que te compres una torta en el camino*", I was like grandma a *torta* doesn't cost five hundred pesos, but that was her way of expressing gratitude for the time I spent with them, with my heart full and tears in my eyes I accepted her gift.

Being able to see all these new perspectives was really a

matter of being open to the experiences, of being open to transformation, and having faith in the lesson I was receiving. I was often questioned on how I managed to live out in the rancho for so long and if I actually enjoyed it. For me, it was a matter of finding happiness in the small details— the beauty of nature in the day to day, the loving kindness of people, the simplicity of life, the understanding of others. It was a matter of having faith, that everything I needed was being provided for. Of embodying the *"Primero Dios"* mentality and really having faith in God and the endless possibilities.

❧ 7 ❧

COME BIEN MIJA

"Me da 20 tacos de asada
Un pozole con patitas de puerco
Ah! Y un refresco grande de dieta
Es que quiero adelgazar!"

— Banda Fresa, *La Dieta*

Every morning, I would wake up as soon as the sun rose and filled my room with light. I would walk over to the kitchen, put on a pot of boiling water and a stick of *canela* and let the room fill with the aroma of cinnamon. I would then proceed to make our breakfast. I would ask my abuela what I should make for breakfast, and she would humbly say *"Huevos con frijoles, papas con huevos, o huevo a huevo. Porque que mas hay?"* and then she would laugh because we always had some kind of egg dish for breakfast. I think she saw life in America as so grand that she couldn't fully understand why I had chosen to go live in México. But I would always tell her, "I'm eating better here than I ever did back home." Breakfast in México was always eggs with salsa, or *carne con papas*, all with a side of *frijoles* and *queso fresco* freshly made by one of our neighbors. Every morning, my *abuelo* would be the first one up to wait for the *tortillas* to be delivered. I still dream about how delicious the food was: eggs from the chickens in the backyard with yolks so yellow that you wonder what you've been eating your entire life in the U.S., tortillas so soft, fresh, and flavorful that you could almost taste the sunlight that helped the corn grow, potatoes so fragrant that they fill up the kitchen when you sauté them in the morning, peppers so spicy that you only had to use a tiny one to give the salsa a good kick. The food here was a different experience that made me appreciate what real food tastes like— this was farm to table, and this was only breakfast.

For lunch we would often make some type of *caldo*, either *caldo de res* or *caldo de pollo*. These stews made the house smell like home, as if you were just wrapped in a blanket of the delicious comforting smells and the warmth this soup would bring to your soul. The food was so flavorful that when I came back to California and had my mom's *caldo de pollo*, it tasted like water in comparison to the rich *caldo* in México. I would eat so well and would never miss a meal— *desayuno*, *comida*, and *la cena* because my abuela would always say, "*Come bien, mija. Sírvete mas.*" She was urging me to put more food on my plate. There wasn't a day that I didn't enjoy my meal, so grateful as I savored every single bite of it. I took it all in, and in the process, I learned how to cook.

My abuela is semi-paralyzed on her left side, which meant that most of the cooking was left to my *abuelo* until I arrived. Now that they had me there, I was making all the intricate dishes— *chile rellenos, enchiladas, espinazo*. I was there to learn, and my abuela was happy to teach me. She gave me direction on what ingredients to add and how to cook them. Every now and again, I would have her taste it, and then I would follow and taste it myself, recognizing the differences in flavor. Through this process, I learned when food tasted bitter, when it needed more salt, when it needed more spice, and when it was just right. I learned that the basis of a lot of Mexican meals is tomatoes, onions, and garlic, and a lot of the salsas are tomatoes, *chiles*, and salt. I learned to tell apart a lot of the *chiles*, dried and fresh, and I learned how to make a variety of salsas. In the kitchen, I recognized the creativity that comes with living in a humble household, how to get creative with left overs and make a new dish, or how to get creative with what you have and make a masterpiece, or how to remix the same dish by using a new salsa.

One of my happiest days cooking was when we made *chiles rellenos*. For whatever reason, growing up as kid, I never liked *chile* or anything spicy; neither did any of my sisters. We ate everything bland. Thankfully I grew out of it, sadly my sisters haven't. The day we made *chiles rellenos* I was reminded of a dish in my childhood— *torrenos*. I remember when I was a little kid my mom would make these; they were slices of boiled potatoes that she would deep fry in a batter. We would love eating these when we were kids. I remember as a kid I would grab one of the chairs from the dining table and bring it close to the stove so I could get a better look at the *torrenos* as they fried in the hot oil. I remember my mom cooking these often, but the last time I remember eating them I was probably still a young kid. When my abuela told me we were going to make them, I got so excited because it reminded me of that young little girl with her chair next to the stove watching her mom make them. Now it was my turn, and I swear I had a smile on my face the entire time I was cooking. Two hours later, we finally sat down and ate, and I enjoyed every single bite of it. The best part was my *abuelo* complementing my cooking and remembering the last time they had *chiles rellenos* because it was too laborious of a meal for them to cook on their own. He said the same thing when I made *enchiladas*, "*Esta rica la comida*." These meals that take lots of time and energy had been missing in my *abuelos'* menu because they could no longer make them on their own, and I was so grateful that I could not only learn but also offer to make it again.

When it came to food in México, I had no reservations. The food was so natural and delicious that rather than thinking of the calories I was thinking of the way it was nourishing my body. I thought about the trees the avocados grew on, the corn and the fields they were picked from, the vast green hills the cows ate from, the fresh milk that the cheese was made from. I had no guilt eating anything in México because it was so natural, and I could feel the satisfaction in my body. This is coming from someone who was vegan the year before! I think with food in México there was the reality that none of it was going to waste and it was mostly local. We would eat our meals, and then we would remix the leftovers, and if there was anything left, the dog would eat it. Every single part of the animal was used in one form or another, so taking an animal's life was not in vain. Being that much closer to the process made me appreciate the food that much more.

I was able to appreciate the dishes I was learning about because there was history in them, a humble history of what my ancestors had to cook as far back as the indigenous communities who passed down the process of *nixtamal*— the first step of softening the corn for making *tortillas*, *tamales*, *atole*. To the salsas being ground and mixed in the *molcajete*. These ingredients indigenous to our land sat so comfortably on my tongue, even if it had been a flavor I had never had before, it was like awakening a new sense that had been neglected for so long. I tried a lot of new dishes, but I still had my limits. Even in just observing, I learned about the humility in our cuisine watching my abuela eat the chicken feet and chicken liver in her *caldo*, telling me about her mom making *torrenos* with pig's feet. I wasn't down to try those, but I appreciated the stories. I did try *espinazo*, which is made of pig spine, and let me tell you that it is one of the most delicious dishes I learned to make.

I was enjoying all the homed-cooked meals but I also enjoyed a lot of the street food México had to offer. *Gazpachos*, Mexican ice cream, *carnitas*, tacos of all kinds, *agua de coco con nuez*, *piñas locas*, garbanzos, *cañas*, an endless amount of snack food, one food concoction more impressive than the last and the best thing about it was none of it came with a side of guilt. There was no need to because there was no constant imagery of perfection. There were no billboards on the roads in the ranchos portraying an unrealistic expectation of beauty like there are in the U.S.; if you watched TV it was rare, and when you did watch it actors often reflected the general public, they looked like my family with a few very attractive people sprinkled in between. There was no sense of perfectionism. The concept of body image here wasn't like that of America, rather it was that of embrace your *lonjas*! And enjoy your food— *come bien*!

Along with food, there was also the satisfaction of music. Every celebration and practically every day, there was something to celebrate. It would be rare to go into town and not hear live music coming from the church or passing through the town square. *Tamborazo* was the soundtrack of the rancho, and every time I would hear it, it was like my heart started beating to the rhythm of the drums and my feet started moving to the beat of the song and my whole body was overcome with joy as I spun to the chorus and let my soul dance freely. This was the beauty of *tamborazo*; it was timeless. I would see six-year-old kids jumping up and down to the beat of "*Camarón Pelado*," and I would go to the high school and see all the teenagers dancing in groups or in couples to the sound of the *banda*. Old couples at the fiestas danced like they were young again. This music encompassed all generations across time and there was no one who didn't enjoy it!

I remember the day I was at my cousins' high school for *Día de Los Muertos*, and the whole school was dressed in traditional *guare* attire and the *tamborazo* was playing out in the basketball court. All the ladies wore their vibrant skirts with their colorful blouses spinning to the music and letting their skirts flow through the air, and all the guys wore their *tejanas* and cowboy boots, *zapateando* and stomping to the beat loud enough to let the ground feel the passion they carry in their hearts. The ladies held on tightly as their partner spun them like a cyclone to the rhythm of the beat. Walking through the middle of it all made me wonder what it would have been like to go to high school in México because, from what I could tell, this dance was more fun than my prom. It just held a different level of passion, one that you could only find in the motherland.

This was the importance of being there in person, tasting the food and letting it fill my body, listening to the music and letting it fill my soul, and being there and open to letting my heart be filled with love. As much as I tried with weekend getaways to Tijuana and my obsession with tacos in L.A., there was nothing comparable to the experience of being in México, and immersing myself in every aspect of it: eating Mexican ice cream every time I went into town, listening to *banda* starting on Monday all the way through the weekend, having every milestone in life celebrated from baptism to marriage and even death. A lot of people when they visit México revel in the beauty of the country, part of that is because of the way people live their lives in México filled with love, humility, passion and joy.

❧ 8 ❧

ENTRE GENERACIONES

"Yo tengo los años nuevos
Mi padre los años viejos
El dolor lo lleva dentro
Y tiene historia sin tiempo"

— Piero de Benedictis, *Mi Querido Viejo*

I was sitting in my abuelas living room watching TV. It was an evening in December, and one of my cousins had come for a visit. She was born in México but was now living in the states, the mother of three young children all under the age of four and she had brought them to visit their *bisabuelos*. Both my *abuela* and my *abuelo* lit up when they saw the kids; they were so happy to have the little ones running around the kitchen yelling and playing, bringing life to the house. They beamed with joy as they held the little ones in their arms, giving them kisses and speaking in baby-talk. Seeing my *abuelos* happy made me happy. They loved seeing their great-grandchildren, and they loved seeing their grand-children too. While appreciating that moment, I realized that there were four generations of the Hernández family in that room. My *abuelos*, my *tío*, my *primas* and I, and my little nieces. What a blessing to have so many generations in one room.

As I watched those little girls running around in all different directions, I gave props to my cousin for raising three toddlers, all while younger than me! Seeing the little girls running around in their little pigtails, playing with each other and then fighting as sisters do, made me recognize that this was what me and my siblings were like. In that moment, I realized that I had never given my mom enough credit for raising so many kids so close together in age, and in a different country with little to no help because of the distance from the rest of her family.

I was able to recognize that my *prima* is where my parents were twenty years ago. She was now the one raising her kids in a new country where she doesn't know the language. She is now the one who takes those long road trips in December and brings her kids down to México, year after year, for the fiestas, dressing them up as *guares*, and having them connect with their family here. These little girls, my nieces, were me and my siblings twenty-five years ago, enjoying their time running around grandma's house, being loved by all the extended family, and spending time with *tíos* and *tías* they only get to see once a year. I was now that *tía* that they would only see during family reunions in México. I realized that my generation now had the responsibility to keep those traditions alive. I also recognized that, besides me, my sisters, and one cousin, there was no one else who traveled to the rancho; everyone else had stopped coming. It had been more than a decade, almost two for some, since they had come. Some of my nieces and nephews did not even know who all their *tíos* and *tías* were.

That blew my mind, and it made me appreciate my

parents for always making us *saludar* the *visita* when people came to visit and for introducing us all around the *rancho* when we were younger. At the very least, we were introduced and knew of our extended family. What's funny is that when I was a kid, I used to hate it because I was so shy and socially awkward. Most of the time when we had guest over I hid in my room until they all left. Being in México and being open to all experiences, I recognized that my parents had taught me some of the best networking skills known to man. In México I was now all about the *platica*, having *visita* over, meeting all my *abuelos'* guests.

Now, when the phone rang at my abuela's house I was the one to pick up the call and chat with whoever was on the line. I would introduce myself and ask how they were doing, and they would ask how my family was doing and tell me about the time they met me when I was younger, and they would ask me how I was liking the *rancho* and how everyone was doing out there. I would be on the phone for a good five minutes before I passed on the phone to my *abuela*. I was speaking to family in Texas, Idaho, California, and I realized how far our network of family extended. I also realized that my abuela had better social ties than I did. I know I've been blessed with amazing friends, but none of them call me every week and spend time catching up like that. I was like, "Get it, Grandma! People love you!"

I noticed this more and more as time went on. She would have visitors checking in on her and my *abuelo* to see how they were doing. In days where we would sit outside by the front door to soak up the sun, we would have people who knew my *abuelos* pass by and stop to say hello. There was almost never a day where I wouldn't see my *abuelo* chatting it up with a friend while he was sitting outside. I would hear stories of how much people loved my *abuela* and the good times they would have visiting her when she had her store.

Several times, I heard stories of my dad and my uncles and what they were like when they were younger.

One of my favorite experiences was when I went into town with my *abuelo*. We were taking care of a few errands, and as soon as my *abuelo* walked up to the *plazuela*, I heard all the men left and right greeting him— "*Buenos días Cheque*," "*Como esta Cheque*," "*Que le damos Cheque*," "*No le vendo una paleta Cheque*." I felt like I was walking with the most popular kid at school. I remember my grandpa turning to me and telling me he didn't know who some of those men were, and I just laughed. I thought to myself, "Dang, Grandpa, you famous!". I asked my dad about this, and he told me that back in his prime my *abuelo* was a popular store owner— not only that but he also raised livestock and was well known in the community. I was getting VIP treatment just by association. When we got to the butcher, he greeted my *abuelo* with respect and asked, "*Que le doy Cheque?*"— asking what kind of meat we wanted, and he made sure to mention he was giving us the best cuts. After that day, the butcher knew whose granddaughter I was, and he continued to hook us up with the best cuts of meat on the market. The same thing happened with the grocer, whom my *abuelo* had known as a kid growing up.

Everywhere we went, everyone had respect and reverence for my *abuelo*, and I was reaping the benefits of it. Was this what it felt like to be a legacy child? How lucky was I to have this experience in the place my grandparents called home. It was nice to get this new insight into the lives of my elders that I never knew about. I was grateful, and I recognized that I had so much to learn from these individuals. How lucky was I to be there and give myself the time to do it while they are still alive.

This reminded me of a conversation I had with a friend. She mentioned that the U.S. was one of the few countries where only nuclear families lived together. Most cultures around the world had three generations or more of family in a household, and México was definitely one of them. My friend brought up the fact that having grandparents was a benefit mostly to the children because they had an extra set of adults to give them attention when parents were too busy with work, additionally, the grandparents could share their wisdom and unconditional love. That resonated because I was learning so much from my *abuelos* every single day, and they loved me so unconditionally just for being me. They didn't care if I had a job, they just cared that I was there. I noticed that during my first couple of months both of my *abuelos* would not want me to do too much around the house so I would be comfortable during my stay. I would always tell them, "*Como que deje el quehacer?*"— when they would suggest I leave the chores for them. They had this association that chores would be too much work for myself alone, but I actually loved doing them— more than anything I loved doing it for them.

After I got back from my three-week break in California, I noticed that my grandma had this renewed sense of energy. I think she was expecting the worst and thinking I wouldn't come back to finish off the year with them. She was always concerned that I would think life was too rough in the rancho given the luxuries in California, so when she saw me come back again, she was so excited to have me that she started doing more around the house— not that I needed her to, but her doctor had recommended she stay active around the house. Every morning after breakfast, she would now get up off her wheelchair and help me clean the kitchen. I would even see her grab the mop and move it around as she went through the kitchen on her wheelchair; of course the wheels of the chair would leave streaks on the floor, but I would get to those later when she took her afternoon nap. Just as much as I appreciated being there with my *abuelos*, I could tell that they also loved having me there as well. It gave them something to look forward to. They often told me how they loved that the house didn't feel so lonely anymore. My heart was always full when I was with them especially every time they expressed their love with their kind words.

As much as this was true, my *abuela* would always push me to hang out with my friends on a daily basis. I felt like a kid again being told to go out and play. One night when we were at my *abuelos*, my *abuela* called for my friend Mariana. I told her, "*Te habla mi abuela*," feeling like a kid saying my grandma wants to talk to you. My abuela wanted to tell her how glad and appreciative she was that she came by our house and to come by more often so I don't spend the day sitting at home being bored. I replied to my *abuela*, "*Ay, y quien dijo que estaba aburrida?*" I had been enjoying the peace, tranquility, and their company, and my grandma thought I just sat around at home being bored. But it was a nice thought, and I appreciated my grandma being so gracious to my friend.

It was my new friends in México that taught me to really be present and enjoy each other's company and the importance of unfiltered laughter. There was one night when we where hanging out on the roof just chatting and looking at the stars and we noticed a flickering light in the sky and my funniest friends Walter and Steven would make the most hilarious commentary about it being a night club in the sky because God was happy and was throwing a party which had us dying of laughter, the kind of laughter that made your cheeks hurt and gave you an ab workout. Or the moments when Estrella would be scrolling through Facebook making commentary on everyones pictures and also those moments when she would put me on blast with the *chisme*. Anyone who has been around a group of Mexicans understand how savage their humor is, but the great thing about it is that no one takes in personally because at the end of the day everyone will always be there for you.

Which brings me to the other trait my friends carried, they were all truly loving and supportive individuals. The way Mariana, Dulce, Estrella and Steven cared for every animal they came across, especially the stray dogs. They once bought bread and had me slow down the car when they saw a dog on the street so they could toss a piece for it to eat. Also the way in which each of them helped support their mom in her food stand and how my cousin Dari did the same helping my *tía* run her store and delivering *tamales* all through the *rancho*. I noticed they all carried this sense of light-heartedness that most young people in the U.S. don't often have and they all carried this sense of wisdom and purpose. They understood that the most important things in life were family, community and friendships. Which is why it was no surprise that as young as they were they still shared so much wisdom. Some of the best advice I ever got was from my 16-year old cousin.

Making new friends in México and simply hanging out was a good change of pace. While I was in México, I re-read the memoir *Top Five Regrets of the Dying* where it discussed how we tend to be products of our environments. I definitely noticed the difference hanging out with my *abuelos* compared to hanging out with the young kids. With my *abuelos*, life was a slower pace; it was about history and reflection and wisdom. With the younger kids, it was about living, having fun, being active, making mistakes. We spent one of those days playing basketball, and I realized how out of shape I was, huffing and puffing as my cousin Dari was making shots all around me, even passing the ball in between my legs to make the shot. My abuela was right— going out with the teenagers was a good idea because they kept me young.

I was appreciative of the balance of life, old and new. I could experience both here to their fullest authenticity, and I noticed this even more so as time went on. In December during the posadas, we would all gather around and go to the houses to sing, celebrate, and eat in anticipation for Christmas. The whole rancho would come out to this, the young kids especially and even the teenagers to collect their goody bags. All the *señoras* would set up the nativity, sing, pray, and pass out food after the celebration. What I witnessed during these times was the concept of "it takes a village to raise a child." I saw the little kids playing with the candles we lit while we sang, melting the wax onto the floor and molding it in between their fingers to entertain themselves. Instead of being with their moms, they would gather around with the teenagers who would keep a watchful eye to make sure they didn't burn or hurt themselves. I thought about the last time I had seen teenagers take care of a bunch of kids willingly, and I couldn't think of it. This happened often; we would be sitting outside hanging out by the fire, and there might be one or two kids who wanted to be around our company. It made me recognized how age segregated my life had been since I spent the majority of my time with adults, I was able to appreciate the wisdom of my elders and the curiosity of the kids and learn a little bit from both.

This sense of community was more and more apparent as time went on. During December, so many people were coming to México to visit their families, which meant all kinds of food. It was at this time that I learned how to cook *pozole*. The first thing about cooking *pozole* is you have to make enough for all your family and neighbors. I learned this from my mom who, every time she made *pozole*, would make it in a pot that could fit ten gallons of food. When it was done, we would take a pot to each of my aunts who lived on our block. This didn't change in México. The pot was so big that we would use the gas stove outside in the *jacal*, and we would have to use a three-foot wooden spoon to stir the pot.

Mind you, it was only my grandparents and I, but we made enough to share with the whole rancho. At one point, we made *pozole*, and one of the neighbors brought us some of her *pozole*, so we just mixed it in with ours. We had so much *pozole* that even the dog was eating *pozole* for weeks, but that's how it is in México, checking on your neighbors and sharing food in celebration.

One of the best pastimes, and probably the most enter-taining things in the rancho were the fiestas. Anyone who was celebrating anything— a marriage, a *quinceañera*, a baptism— put on a fiesta. What was great about it was that it was for the whole rancho, the community. Food would be provided in the daytime, pounds and pounds of delicious *carnitas*, and in the evening the bar vendors would come to provide the drinks and the stage would be set for the *banda* that was going to play all the way into the night. For rural towns in México that don't have a lot of money, these fiestas were often made possible by all those community members who lived *en El Norte*. These fiestas were a way for people who had found success in America to share their wealth in a way that could be enjoyed by the community. The only thing that was expected of the town was for them to come and have a good time. This happed all over the ranchos. If we heard a *banda* from our youth was going to be at another rancho, we would go out to the fiesta, no invitation needed. This is how I managed to see *Banda Machos* and *Arkangel R-15* and reminisce the songs from my childhood that I would dance *quebradita* too when my parents played it from a boombox in our back-yard family parties.

There's so much pride in representing the rancho you come from because there's not much to flaunt other than the fiestas they put on. There's this humility of being poor, but there is no shame associated with it, which is why everyone celebrates everything. This was community, and I think my parents did a good job in keeping those traditions in the states. I grew up in a block where my neighbors were my family members; it was like they wanted to recreate the rancho in our block. I grew up taking pots of food to my tías across the street and returning Tupperware at random hours of the day. We would take food to each other and visit unannounced. We would have family parties and celebrate all life's milestones. As kids we would always be running around on the street playing games and telling each other jokes and our aunts and uncles would always be outside watching over us as they watered their lawns. That's how I grew up, but the only place I've experienced that now was in México.

The intergenerational experience is rare in America. We segregate ourselves by our age so much that we often don't give a chance to what we can learn from others, even kids. This was probably one of the reasons I was so overwhelmed and stressed with work, because I didn't give myself enough time to spend with kids who make you feel care-free or with elders who remind you of what really matters in life. One thing for sure is that people never sit back and reminisce about all the extra hours they put in at work, they sit back and think of all those moments where their heart was full or their stomach ached of all the laughter and good times they shared with others. I was glad I was able to do that every day in México. In a sense my *rancho* was the village that raised me in those few months I was there. They taught me about all the *costumbres* I had lost in the U.S. and I was grateful that they helped me learn them again by simply being present with me.

❧ 9 ❧

SE COMO UN ÁRBOL

CRECE HACIA EL SOL Y SIEMPRE FIEL A TUS RAÍCES

"I feel very proud to be Mexican. I didn't have the opportunity to learn Spanish when I was a girl, but it's never too late to get in touch with your roots."

— Selena Quintanilla

I was in the kitchen with my *abuelos*. We had just spent the morning eating breakfast and listening to my *abuelo* tell me some of his life stories. He went on to tell me how back in the day he would eat everything when they had their store, from fruits, vegetables and beans of all kinds. They went far and wide to make sure their store was stocked with a variety of food and supplies. They would drive all over Michoacán to buy *comales de barro*, wooden spoons as tall as your legs, and the best produce on the market. He said it with so much pride that I knew my *abuelo* worked hard to provide not only for his family but for the community given that he went and bought artisanal items to have in stock for the rancho. He would talk about how people around the rancho would share the large wooden spoons when cooking and they would pass them around from house to house, especially when making carnitas, and how people would always come to the store and ask for the special cooking pots and utensils because he would be the only one who would offer them.

He continued on to tell me that when my dad was young, he would send him out to the soccer field down by the *parcelas* where the kids would play sports to sell fruit and sodas. He told my dad to go out and hustle at least so he could have some money in his pocket since they couldn't provide much. At the time, they were putting their eldest son through university, and they didn't have much money to spare. So my dad would go out with his piles of fruit and sodas to sell. With him out there in the field, he developed some friendships, and they either helped him carry his merchandise, helped sell it, or bought some on the field.

My abuelo also mentioned how much my *tías* would help around the store when they were younger. My abuelo said *"Las muchachas siempre nos ayudaban en la tienda cuando se ofrecía, especialmente cuando había fiesta porque se llenaba la tienda."* He had such an appreciative look in his eyes when he talked about and remembered how much my *tías* would help around the house when he and my grandma would spend all day working in the field. There were times where my *abuelos* were so busy with work, either harvesting the fields or buying merchandise, that my tías from a young age had to step up and help around the store. He told me how, more often than not, he and my *abuela* and even my dad would be out harvesting the fields and my *tías* were in charge of running the store and taking care of my youngest *tío* who was still too young to do much of anything. They would also be in charge of making the meals for the family since my *abuelos* were gone most of the day working.

The way both of my *abuelos* talked about their kids and how much they appreciated them for helping out when they were young made my heart warm. I could sense the pride he had for his family in the way he told these stories, and to this day, he appreciated their help so much. We had transitioned to washing the dishes and cleaning the kitchen counter. He was emptying the pans and preparing some food for the dog, and of course being the sap that I am, I tried to dry out the tears in my eyes as I kept washing the dishes. I just got some *chile* in my eyes Grandpa, I swear I'm not crying.

I asked him how young my dad was at the time because I knew that he wanted to go to the states in his early teens. He said he was twelve or thirteen because, soon after, my dad started talking about wanting to go out to the states and work. My *abuelo* had his brother Donato— we knew him as *Papa*— out here, and he was helping my dad arrange how to get to California. My *abuelo* mentioned how things became hard after my dad left since they no longer had him to help out in the fields given that my other *tío* was still too young to work, but he understood why my dad had left because there was only so much they could provide for him here in México. He said my dad wanted better clothes since he would be running around with holes in his pants. My *abuelo* then mentioned how back in the day people wore out their pants; they wore them torn out of necessity, and today people wear torn pants "*de lujo*." He knew they couldn't provide what my dad wanted, even if it was a simple pair of new pants, because they were providing for my *tío* at university. Since he was out in the city, my *tío* needed to be more presentable, whereas the rest of the kids were out in the rancho where everyone would be running around in raggedy clothes so it didn't matter so much. So off my dad went at fourteen years old to try to earn a better living in the U.S.

It's stories like these that open my eyes to another part of history that I never knew about. It allows me to see both my dad and my *tías* and *tíos* as children, and it allows me to see my grandparents as parents. They have their own family history, and I can see how that has in one way or another influenced how we were raised. For one, we all ended up in the states to live a better life. I can say for sure that I never had to work the field or wear raggedy clothes unless I was playing out in the mud. Through these stories, I'm able to see the transition from generation to generation, and it's amazing to see how far we've come. Stories like these made me so grateful that I took a chance on myself taking the time to reconnect. Every time I heard a story like this— and there were plenty of them— it filled my heart to know and understand that I came from such greatness, not just in my culture but in my family.

Another time, my *abuelo* started talking about the *parcelas* he owned down the road from the house. He said he had them divided up for each of his children, and he started talking about the land his father owned. He told me be about the time my *bisabuelo*, my great-grandfather who happened to be an alcoholic, took my *tío*, the youngest one in the family, to the community meetings. People in the community were complaining that my *bisabuelo* wasn't being responsible enough to come and represent himself in the meetings, so he took my uncle who was a pre-teen at the time. He presented my uncle as the new representative on his behalf, and everyone objected because of his age. My *bisabuelo* then said, "*Como no va estar mejor, si yo y todos ustedes ya estamos viejos y solo vamos pa' abajo y el que esta joven so lo va pa' arriba.*" He was questioning why they objected if they were all old and had nowhere to go but downhill with age while my uncle who was young could only go uphill. So that was my uncle's introduction to the community, and to this day, I see how involved he is and continues to be. This all really made me appreciate the beauty of the small town and the sense of community involvement. I also see it with my *primo*— his son— who spends

83

MAIRA HERNÁNDEZ

most of his time with all the other young men, drinking beer but also planning the rodeo every year and pitching in financially for the biggest town celebration.

It was during this conversation that I started to ask more about how my *abuelo* came to live in this house. He mentioned that originally the land belonged to one of his brother's, but he was *en El Norte* and wasn't using it, so when he and my grandma got married, they started building a house. He said he built it with his own hands, making bricks the *adobe* and bringing the *tierra* to mix it and build it from the ground up. It took a few weeks, but finally, they were able to move into the small house, which consisted of a small room with just a mattress. He told me he kept expanding the house little by little and even helped build the school next door. Looking at my *abuelos'* house now, I look at it with more appreciation knowing that they built it themselves. When I look at both my *abuelos'* hands, I can see so much strength and hard work, and I'm so proud to come from such a hardworking family. I see their house and picture it only being one little room compared to the five rooms and kitchen that they now have, and I'm able to appreciate all the hard work that it took to build. I can see the *adobe* bricks in between the doorways; they have now been covered with cement and painted over, but in between the doors lies the memory of the house they built with their hands.

As the days went on, whenever there was a conversation like this, I took it upon myself to be intentional and ask the right questions to learn more about my family history. I asked my grandma about the store they used to own; now it was just a storage room but it still held the memories of my childhood. As a child when we would come to México, we would love to be in my abuelas house because we had what seemed like an unlimited supply of candies, soda, and chips. I still remember where she had my favorite lollipops and the drawer where she kept the change. My cousins and I would always take turns playing cashier and give each other change for the candies we bought with our pesos. I asked my abuela how long had it been since they closed down their *tiendita*. It happened once my abuela started having health problems. She began to realize that keeping the store would not be the best idea. She would have trouble giving back correct change and even giving the right items people were asking for. There was even a kid who would mess around with her, either taking items or poking holes in the bread and ruining the items she could sell. My abuela caught him and told him that she didn't care if it was just five pesos worth, he was going to respect her and her store and she gave him the opportunity to pay for it or she was going to take him to talk to his dad and tell him what he had been up to. So he paid up— I felt proud of my *abuela* for handling this kid.

My *abuelos* got along with all the people they bought their merchandise from and with all their customers. In his prime, my *abuelo* was a store owner, he raised livestock, and he planted and harvested his land. He was in the business of providing what was necessary in the town to provide for his family. He and my *abuela* were so well-liked that all the merchandisers would sell to my *abuelo* at a discounted price. He had such good relationships that even if he didn't have the money to pay for all the merchandise, they would give him the flexibility to pay the next time.

All in all, with the stories I've heard from my *abuelos* and seeing first-hand how much respect and reverence people in the rancho and the neighboring towns have for them, I could see how successful they were in their days. For them, it was important to have great relationships with everyone they worked with, and they saw the benefit of that with the loyalty of their customers and merchants. Not only that but they had respect for their store and their work, and they demanded it

MAIRA HERNÁNDEZ

from those who tried to take advantage. I see those same qualities in my dad and in his way of raising us. There's a certain respect he commands just in his being, but he is also the most reasonable and calm person that I know. I'd like to think that my siblings and I have gained some of those qualities ourselves, and I can see how that gets passed down from generation to generation.

There were so many experiences I had in México that made me realize the importance of staying connected to the motherland. The most important one was understanding my elders as complex individuals, compared to the one-dimensional identity I saw them in before. My *abuela* was both a mother, a wife, a daughter, a tía, a friend. I saw the same in my *abuelo*. For the longest time, I had just seen my *abuelos* as my grandparents, but they were more than that. Being in the motherland allowed me to see that they didn't just belong to me and my family; they also belonged to the community they came from.

I continued to recognize this, and I would always have a moment with elders in the community who would ask me about my family. One of these moments was when I met my other abuela's best friend, and she would tell me stories of them spending time together walking from one *rancho* to another. I felt so special knowing that I had met one of my *abuela's* best friends, and I was lucky enough to hear stories from when they were young. This also happened when I would introduce myself to elders in the *rancho*. They immediately knew whose daughter I was by the features that I carried from my parents. This is why I firmly believe that people from the rancho could be amazing cultural anthropologists because one look at you and they could tell what family you came from. As I traveled to other states in México, I would often see some people who oddly reminded me of friends back home and come to find out that they had origins in those particular states in México I was visiting. It was amazing to me that I could travel all over the motherland and see the connections people had across borders, even if they didn't know they existed. How lucky was I to know how far these roots stretched?

✣ 10 ✣

DONDE COME UNO, COMEN DOS

"¡Mientras yo esté aquí no les faltará un taquito!"

— La India María

It was one of my first nights in México, my dad had flown in with me, and we were getting ready for *la cena*. I was heating up dinner. My uncle walked in when we were half-way through eating, and I asked him if he was hungry and if I should heat him up some food. My dad said, *"Como que si quiere? Tu no mas sírvele"*— he said I shouldn't ask I should just serve him a plate. Which made me think of all of the times I would go to a *tías* house and have them tell me to sit down and eat even if I wasn't hungry. Even if I tried to decline the offer, they would still serve me food. A lot of us Latinos look back at this with heartfelt nostalgia of always being taken care of by the women in our families, and here I was asking rather than just doing. This is when I realized that it was now my turn to be that person. Next time, I'm just gonna serve for the simple fact of taking care of someone I care about. As time went on, that's exactly what I did, especially for my *abuelos* and my friends who would visit me at my abuela's house.

While I was in México, I learned how to throw down in the kitchen, and I feel so grateful for that. I hold these recipes in my heart, and one of my greatest joys was serving my *abuelos* and having them enjoy my cooking. I realized that what I loved about cooking was not just cooking an amazing meal but being able to share it with others. So when I came back, I wanted to do the same. I had always been the daughter that would cook for my dad if my mom wasn't around. To this day, I will continue to do that because my dad has worked so hard and continues to work long hours to provide for his family. When I was younger, I would draw a line at serving my brother. I would serve my dad, but my brother could serve himself. That was my feminist stand against machismo.

Coming back from México, I had a new perspective. I genuinely loved to cook. There was an art and a science to making sure all the ingredients came together perfectly, and one of my greatest joys was having my *abuelo* say, "*Quedo bien rica la comida.*" This was my ninety-year-old grandpa who has been eating Mexican food for almost a century, and I just got his stamp of approval. That was it, now I can include my cooking skills on my resume.

Cooking for my *abuelos* and serving them was one form of love that I expressed for them. I now recognized it was the same for my mom and my *tías* and all the matriarchs in our families. I always understood that Mexican mothers express their love through cooking. I remember being off in college and coming back home to a feast. Oftentimes, it was *pozole* or *enchiladas*. Growing up, *pozole* was a once-a-year feast during the holidays. Who knew that all it took was going off to college to get it more often throughout the year? I see the same thing with my abuela. When my dad was around, she had me cooking all of my dad's favorite dishes and then some because he was home for a visit. Just goes to show, you will always be spoiled by your momma no matter how old you are.

When I came back to the states, I wanted to share what I had been taught by my abuela. The sad part was that none of my sisters like *chile*, so there were limited options, at least for my family. But it was still a nice feeling of being able to cook for them as they made jokes, asking questions about all the recipes I learned in my study-abroad experience in the *rancho*. There was another time when I visited my parents for a weekend and only my dad and brother were home. So I made breakfast. I had already served my dad, and I called my brother over and prepared his plate and was preparing my own. Being that he was already used to me not serving him, he was opening the cupboard to grab a plate when I told him the plate sitting on the counter was his. I was happy to cook and fix the plates because of my new chef skills that I learned from my abuela, but I still drew the line at taking his plate to the table because of #Feminism; only my dad earned that special treatment. Having been in the rancho for so long, I understood the gender roles associated with this and I knew that I preferred to work in the kitchen. I wasn't about to go and work in the fields where all the insects, scorpions, and snakes lived, so I was okay with serving a plate after a hard day's work in the field for any man in México. But it was different here in the U.S.

But this brings up a good point. Having learned so many customs that are considered old-fashioned and outdated in the U.S., how do I now blend what I learned to what's acceptable in my modern life? The determining factor for me was to do what allowed me to express my love and gratitude to those I care about.

The biggest lesson I learned was that the kitchen was a place of sharing— sharing food, sharing stories, and spending time together with those that you love. I learned about the hospitality of my culture and how it was up to me to continue this with my own modern flair. So as I went back to the U.S., all I wanted to do was cook for my friends, share with them what I had learned, share a meal together, and build community. Whenever I had the chance, I would be happy to cook a meal and share stories of my many adventures, as well as learn more about my friends as I did so many times with my *abuelos* while we sat at the dinner table. Now that I had such an amazing experience to share, it was easy to have conversations. I once found myself talking to a friend's mom who happened to be from Michoacán, and we bonded over the rancho life and how good the food is over there and how it's hard to get the flavor of a *caldo de pollo* from el rancho. It was also very easy for me to talk to my *tíos* and *tías* about México as I could now relate to them missing their motherlands.

One of my favorite things to do was share more of the culture with my niece and nephews. There was a weekend when they had come to visit us at my parent's house, and I was watching YouTube videos of México and the artisanal culture. My niece came into my room and was curious about what I was watching, so she sat there and watched with me. The video was of a woman making tamales from *nixtamal* using the *metate*, and I would point to the video and explain to my niece what everything was and how this was something we cooked in México and that her great-grandma had a *metate* at home. That same day, I had also pulled out the *molcajete* that I brought from México, and I taught her how to use it and had her practice grinding grains of rice.

This took place during Thanksgiving break, and I remember one of my niece and nephews' homework assignments was on the pilgrims, so I took it upon myself to teach them a little bit about Native Americans and indigenous culture and started sharing pictures of all these ancient cultures and pyramids in México, teaching them how great our history was. This was the first time they had seen pictures of pyramids in México, and they were able to see some of these pyramids in person at the beginning of the new year when we visited Chinchen-Itza. Once I came back to the U.S. after the holiday fiestas were over, I also showed them pictures and videos of my sister and I dressed in our *guare* attire, and I showed them a few pictures of when we were kids their age, dressed in the same traditional attire. It was important to me that they knew about their cultural heritage because when we were their age we were consistently going to the rancho and learning about it firsthand, and though they have been to México, they had never been to the rancho to experience it for themselves.

Just as much as I was sharing my culture and my family history, I also understood that I needed to share more of myself. One of the simplest ways was to add the whole rancho on Facebook. Before, I used to be so meticulous about who I had on my friends list. I didn't want anyone judging me or sharing anything I didn't want my family to see. This time, I understood I was too grown to be posting pictures of partying and too grown to care, and I also understood that it was nice to be connected to the rancho even if it was digitally. So as soon as I started adding a couple of people from the rancho, it wasn't long before everyone and their mommas added me too. It's been nice to continually have interactions with my friends in the rancho. As loving and caring as they are in person, they continue to be so online. I now get most of my likes and supportive comments from the fam in the rancho, which reflects how loving and supportive they were in person. I also noticed that as savage as their humor is in person, it continues to be online, which often brings me to hysterical laughter just when I need it the most.

Being connected to the rancho reminds me so much of

what our parents use to do to keep those traditions alive when we were kids. I remember we constantly had family parties. We would be over a relative's house on a regular basis, going even so far as to drive to distant areas in California just for a visit. I remember our parents making us talk on the phone with people we didn't know. I even remember writing my grandma letters when we were younger. I remember riding my bike with my dad and my *tíos* to the park, and I remember our parents taking us hiking down cliffs by the beach despite the No Trespassing signs that they may or may not have understood. There was more of a sense of adventure, freedom, and of being around each other's company, just because. Every major holiday gave us an excuse for a grand celebration where we all got together, cousins from both sides of the family, and we would all play games and run around being *traviesos*. During birthday parties we had so many cousins that it was always entertaining to see who was going to be the one to smash someone's face on the cake *con la mordida*. I even remember getting home and finishing my homework right away and saying, "*Voy a salir a jugar con los chiquillos*" when telling my mom I was going to go outside and play with my cousins. This was a feeling I knew as a kid and I reconnected to in the rancho when I would hang out with friends, just because, visit family I barely knew, go out and hike *cerros*, and be outside and play with the kids. My parents brought that with them and tried to live to that as much as they could until we grew up and they grew older.

Sure, the times have changed, especially with technology keeping most kids glued to their screens, but in a way, this can make it easier to connect and plan gatherings. Thankfully, I was able to see this play out again over Easter, seeing all my cousins plan a get-together for their kids, all of my nieces and nephews. Sitting back and recognizing that we were now the adults, I saw it was our turn to take the place of our parents.

It is up to us to ride our bikes to the park with the kids, to take them on hikes near the beach like our parents use to when we were young, to plan the holidays where these kids can joy each other's company as *primos*. It is our responsibility to keep the traditions alive, and to do so means taking responsibility and learning more about those traditions. And in many ways, because we are lucky enough to live in a country of cultural diversity, it is also up to us to teach those who are curious about how great our culture is and to include others and be hospitable, just as our families have been with each other. Our traditions are not limited to just family but can be extended to friends, neighbors, and coworkers. The beauty in it all is in the act of sharing because *"donde come uno, comen dos."*

11

NADIE ES ETERNO EN EL MUNDO

"Nadie es eterno en el mundo,
Ni teniendo un corazón.
Que tanto siente y suspira por la vida y el amor."

— Darío de Jesús Gómez Zapata

I don't know anyone who watched Coco and didn't cry in the end as Miguel rushed to get to Mamá Coco before she forgot the memory of her father. That's how I felt when embarking on this journey. I knew there was a treasure that my *abuelos* held in their wisdom, and I only had a limited amount of time to learn about it. The difficult part about this, especially when living in U.S., is coming to terms with the idea that nobody lives forever— "*Nadie es eterno en el mundo*." It seems to me that for us it's easier to go on living life avoiding the inevitable than to take the step into vulnerability in getting to know those in our family who will soon depart. That was the first step of me taking this journey, recognizing that I still had my *abuelos* and that I didn't have all the time in the world.

Death in México is seen differently. We see this in the traditions of *Día de Los Muertos*. We see that the memories of our loved ones are celebrated; they are mourned as well, but more than anything, they are celebrated for the impact they left behind. Before going on this adventure, I only had child-hood memories of my *abuelos*, since they lived in México, I could honestly say that I barely even knew them as people. In the eight year gap of my visits to México I remember talking to my *abuela* on the phone maybe once. That now has changed, and I will forever be grateful that I took the time to know them. In knowing them, I discovered more of myself, in knowing them I became their friend.

I love my *abuelos* so deeply, and I often think about what a loss I'm going to experience the day that they pass. It's going to pain me so much, that just the thought of it brings me to tears. I'm so grateful that I gave myself the time to build a relationship with them and that I not only have those distant memories I had as a child but that I now have the memories and the relationship I built with them as an adult. I'm always going to remember the way my *abuelo* walked so slowly with his cane, using all of his strength to hold on to every shred of independence he still had, walking a few inches at a time but still standing tall— his perfect teeth and perfect vision and the strength in his arms after years and years of working in the fields, all when he was ninety years old. And I will always remember his voice and the way he told stories with so much detail and how he used his hands to narrate these stories, how he would always look at me and then into the distance as he remembered the details of a time long ago.

I'll remember my abuela and how she always had a sense of humor and would make me laugh, often at her expense. How her head would often have a tremor shaking back and forth, a symptom of her Parkinson's and she would say, "*Mira yo aquí siempre diciendo que no,*" and she would laugh about it and make me laugh in the process cracking a joke about how her Parkinson's always had her saying "no." She also always talked about her desire to work, and she would use all of her strength to get up off her wheelchair and help me with chores, and I now will often think of her when I need motivation to get out of my bed to go to work. Now that I'm back in the states, I often think of the way she answers the phone every time I call and how she always tells me, "*Me da mucho gusto que me hables y te acuerdes de mí, cuando escucho tu voz siento que estas aquí*" expressing her gratitude when I call and also giving me the space to express mine when I tell them I miss them too, "*Yo también los extraño y los quiero mucho.*" I'm grateful for these phone calls because my abuela has now become the person who I call whenever I need a little motivation because her kind and loving words always fill my heart. She always sends me blessings and good thoughts and shares memories of our time together in México.

When you're at that age, living life mostly alone with many of your loved ones in distant places, pride no longer exists when expressing love. She expresses it so kindly and openly, especially as I share every aspect of my life, and this has allowed me to express my love for them as well. My phone calls with her were crucial when I moved to a new city after coming back from México and as I started my job search. Not only did those phone calls help me imagine I was back in her kitchen sitting next to her as we shared another meal together, but she would give me so much encouragement that I would always know I would be okay. She would tell me, "*Le pido a Dios que te encuentres un buen trabajo y que puedas ahorrar y que te dejen visitar otra vez,*" she would pray I would find a good job so I can save and visit again soon. I have no doubt that her prayers and wishes for me were the reason that I was blessed with such an amazing job when I got back, even after eight months of being unemployed. As I shared that with her, she would say, "*Me da mucho gusto que te haigas encontrado un buen trabajo y que estés feliz.*" What did I do to deserve such a love so pure? As I write this, I'm crying because I miss my *abuelos* so much, but I also recognize that these tears are a part of the process. The walls that I had around my heart that kept me from visiting or even having a simple phone call started to shatter in my journey to México, and those walls continue to break as my heart expands and lets in all this love that was meant for me and even more so as I continue to share it with others.

This is why I found it so important when I got back to the U.S. to visit my other abuela in Chicago. I knew she wasn't doing well, but I wasn't prepared to see her how she was. Her all-white hair was longer than she'd had it before, and she was smaller than I remembered, her body frail and wrapped in blankets keeping her warm as she took in small shallow breaths. She blinked her eyes to try to keep them open long enough to see who I was.

"*Mamá Amparo, es Maira,*" I said with a sad, forced smile on my face in hopes that she would recognize me.

It took all of me to keep tears from streaming from my eyes, as I forced a smile while looking directly in her eyes. I don't think she recognized me, but spiritually, I felt a connection, and I felt at peace. In that moment, I felt the presences of mi Papá Alvaro and my cousin Cindy as if they were watching over her. As I stood there, I felt sad that I didn't get to hear many stories from Mamá Amparo, that I didn't get to know her as a I did my other abuelos. I was sad that I didn't have more vivid memories of her as a kid, just her and I. The one thing I did remember was that she always prayed; whenever she was staying with us in California I always saw her praying, day and night, for all of us, and I know with all my heart that I was on that list. I knew that as I stared at the rosary hanging on her wall next to her frail body.

As sad as I was in this moment, I was also grateful that I was there. It had been three years since I had last seen my *abuela* when I accompanied her on the flight to Chicago. She was mostly on a wheelchair then but could still get up and use her walker. Back then, she still had color in her hair from the last time she dyed it. My uncle told me that last year her body was weak but her spirits were still high.

She would say, *"Ahorita nos vamos a tomar una tequilita pa' ponernos a bailar"*— saying that they would be taking a tequila shot and getting up to dance.

I wish I could have been there to hear her, but as I pictured that, I heard her laugh as clear as if it were happening in that moment. This time I wasn't so lucky to hear it once more and to share stories from México like I wanted to, I wanted to tell her that I had gotten to know her best friend, but nonetheless I was grateful I was there; grateful that I had spent so much time in México that I had learned to appreciate my *abuelos* so deeply; grateful that everything aligned so perfectly for me to come visit my *abuela* in Chicago; grateful that I was there seeing her breathing and seeing her eyes and seeing her see me smile one last time; grateful that as I left I got to give her one last kiss on her forehead.

As my flight took off from Chicago, a wave of sadness took over me. I recognized that this might be the last time I see my Mamá Amparo alive. I spent a good hour just crying like a *mocosa* as I looked out of the window into the clouds feeling all my feelings of sadness, gratitude and love. I recognized that this journey wasn't easy, but it was necessary. With life being what it is in the U.S. and with her health deteriorating, I knew the next time I would see my abuela would be when she passed. My *tíos* have arranged for that day to have her remains transported to México, her final resting place with mi Papá Alvaro. That is how strong the roots of México are: that a good number of people want to be returned to their motherland for their final resting place. Even though I wasn't born there, I myself would prefer to be buried there. Especially knowing how both life and death are celebrated in México.

The celebration of *Día De Los Muertos* helped me realize this. For the first time in my life, I was in México during this important holiday. I was able to see everything from the fields of *cempasúchil*, the bright orange marigolds, covering various acres around the *cerros* of Michoacán to the flowers being harvested on the days before the holiday, to then being sold in bulks in the *plazas* and seeing children and teenagers alike with their faces painted as *calaveras*. I bought some *cempasúchil* for my Papá Alvaro's tomb, and I printed some pictures that I had of him. I remember the last time I had visited his tomb, almost ten years before, I still felt a little sad for the loss. This time, it was a day of celebration, and I couldn't help but run through the memories I had of my grandpa. I always remember him being happy and joyful when he would have us around. He would always take us to the store to buy candy or ice cream, and as we would walk through the town, he would always walk with his hands behind his back in a stroll, taking in the sights of his rancho. More than anything I remember his laugh. Given that I have gotten to know my other *abuelos* so much, I wondered about all the stories I didn't know about mi Papá Alvaro. But I was glad to be there that day and pay tribute to him by washing his tomb and decorating his grave on *Día de Los Muertos* with the help of my friend Mariana. I was happy that I was there to do that and even happier to send the pictures of the decorated tomb to my mom, who then sent them to all my *tías* and *tíos*.

Those couple of days of celebration are something I will never forget, from taking time to reminisce the moments

AVENTURA, AMOR Y TACOS

with the ones we've lost, to the mass in the *panteón* paying tribute to all their souls, to the celebration of sharing a meal by their tombs. On a larger scale, my cousins and I were able to see one of the more indigenous towns celebrate it in Tzintzuntzan— un *Pueblo Mágico*. After our rancho's celebration, we headed out and arrived in the evening. We walked through a wooden doorway next to the church that lead to a huge field. It almost looked like a park— trees and grass everywhere. There were small candles and *cempasúchil* lining the long walkways along the grass. It felt like that moment in Coco when Miguel first walks into the Land of the Dead, only better because this was real life and I could hear *banda* everywhere. I was so excited and filled with emotion that I was lucky enough to experience this in none other than the state of Michoacán, my motherland. This was how beautiful my culture was, these are my origins, this was magic!

Off in the distance, we saw the *bandas* and a parade of people making their way out of the church grounds and towards the *panteón*. We were all in awe of how beautiful everything was and the excitement in the air. We made our way towards the crowd, and it was amazing to see the families and the women dressed as *guares* with the indigenous garments used by the *Purépechas*, carrying the corona de *cempasúchil* and the *ofrendas* to be placed in their loved one's tomb. It was one family after another, each with their own *banda*, different songs flowing in the air as the celebration went on. There was so much beauty in this celebration, seeing all these families honoring their loved ones, tombs so intricately decorated and the *panteón* full of festivities with the smell of *cempasúchil* floating in the air.

This is when I recognized the power of my ancestry. Yes, it is going to be heartbreaking mourning the loss of my *abuelos* when the time comes, but it would have been even harder if I had not built a relationship with them and created

the memories that I have now. Not only that but I had assimilated so much to the American culture that I was relying on
an American idea of loss and mourning when in contrary my
ancestors have been celebrating life and death for centuries.
It was important for me to connect to my ancestry and
understand the indigenous influences that play into my
culture. I realized the importance of understanding the timeless wisdom that has been passed down from generation to
generation. It was a reminder that I not only came from
greatness in my family but that I also came from greatness in
the ancestors that built pyramids, built communities, and
built empires and let's not forget, the once who also created
the taco! I had finally tapped into that wisdom in the best
way that I could by connecting to the greatness of my
ancestors.

12

NUNCA VOY A OLVIDARME DEL RANCHO

"Siempre voy a sentir orgulloso
Como extraño sus calles de tierra
Y a las señoras con su rebozos"

— Espinoza Paz, *Calles de Tierra*

When I set off on this adventure, I knew I was going to experience happiness like I never had before. What I didn't know was how much love I was going to receive from all the people who I crossed paths with. To say that I love México and its people is an understatement. So when I finally had to leave the *rancho*, I knew it was going to be one of the more difficult things I ever had to do. I got on the bus with my luggage, and as soon as we drove off, I started to cry— not just a cute little tear streaming down my eye but the ugly *mocosa* cry for how much I was going to miss living there. I knew I'd be back, but I also knew that I probably wouldn't get another long-term experience like this. When experiences as beautiful as this happen, it's always hard to say goodbye.

Which is why, as I sat on the bus with all my luggage watching all the corn fields, *pueblos*, and *cerros* pass me by, I cried about how much harder it must have been for my parents. I was only there five months, and it felt like I was leaving behind the best life I ever lived. I can only imagine what it felt like for my parents to leave the place of their birth, leave behind their friends and family, and go into an unknown country. A sad reality of immigration is that non-immigrants don't understand this idea. I remember a few years ago sitting on my therapist's couch talking about the burden I felt to be successful being a first-generation professional, how I worked extremely hard to go to the best college that I could and to come out of it with a good career to make the sacrifice my parents made worth it.

The therapist then asked me, "What sacrifice?" For a second, I paused and thought to myself, "Is she asking this for real?" I looked at her, waiting for a response, and realized that she was serious.

I responded, "Well they moved to a new country and left their family behind to pursue the American Dream."

She then responded, "It's only a sacrifice when you leave behind something that is better than where you're going."

I looked with a blank stare trying to process what I just heard, and I realized in that moment that I wouldn't be back to see her again.

At the time, I was speechless. I didn't even have a rebuttal because I didn't know how to describe how wrong she was. Maybe it was because I was so disconnected from my memories of México that I could not immediately think of a reason why she was so wrong, but I knew it in my heart she was wrong. This made me realize how lucky I was that my family took on the journey to travel to México every single year. In a distant memory in my childhood, I knew that life in México was great. As a child, you rarely think of finances, but that is the reason my parents migrated to the states. I have always known México was amazing to begin with but given how busy I was with life, I had never given my self the time to let that love blossom into something beautiful. The time and nourishment I gave myself visiting the motherland this time around was all I needed.

I discovered so many life lessons by returning to the motherland my parents had left behind. It was an eye-opening experience for me to not just experience my motherland but to be a witness to the history of my parents' lives as I heard my *abuelos* share stories with me. I fell more deeply in love with México, with my history, with my family, my people, with my *rancho* the more I discovered and the more open I was to receiving these experiences.

Knowing that many people in my communities in the U.S. come from similar backgrounds, I knew this was something I needed to share. It felt as if I had discovered a secret in my ancestry and it would have been selfish to keep it to myself. Besides, one of the things that I learned in my time in México was sharing *con la comunidad*. If I kept my story to myself, I wouldn't be staying true to the lessons I learned.

Being in México was a gift for me. It helped me rediscover myself. It helped me find my joy again. I rediscovered the childlike joy I had in visiting when I was young. It was almost like being in a time machine, going back to the rancho, participating in the *posadas*, dressing up as a *guare* for the fiestas. It took me back to being carefree and that is how I chose to live my life in México— carefree.

What was great about it was also the role my *abuelos* played. They themselves made me feel like a kid again, from telling them where I was going and checking in on the phone every couple of hours, to them staying up until I made it home if I was out at a *baile* at night or even the way that I could do no wrong in their eyes. Those late nights, I would go to my *abuelos* door when I returned from the *baile* and yell, "Abuela! *Ya llegue! Que pasen buenas noches!*" This reminded me of the reassurance every parent needs to make sure you made it home safely. Some people could have looked at my situation and seen an unemployed, emotional wreck, bumming off of her grandparents. For them, I was their granddaughter who had taken time out of her life to spend it with them and take care of them and run errands for them and love them. Giving myself the permission to be that person took tremendous courage and a lot of love. To walk away from everything I had learned in America and return home. For that, I am proud of myself! It's also heartwarming now talking to my abuela over the phone and reminiscing about my time living there, telling me how she will be eternally grateful for the time I spent with them, grateful even after death. Her gratitude fills my heart and makes me realize how worth it this adventure was for me.

I understand that most people can't go on this same adventure and leave all responsibility behind. Which is why my hope is that people will take these bits of wisdom and put them into practice, these *dichos* and lessons we have often heard but have probably forgotten. These insights into our culture and ancestry that have been passed down for many generations but we have maybe not given much thought to. My hope is that with these lessons people gain a new understanding of life, a new understanding tied to their motherland with the plan to visit as soon as possible even if it is for just a week. Imagine putting these lessons into practice and being so prepared to visit your own motherland, that when you actually get the chance to visit you take full advantage of every moment.

Being back in the U.S. hasn't been easy because I miss México every day, but I've put into practice a lot of the lessons I learned because I now understand that those lessons keep me tied to the motherland until the next time I return and I wish the same for you. I wish that if you still have grandparents, that you call them, because even if you haven't talked to them in years you will probably make their day! My abuela still tells me *"Gracias por llamarme, cada vez que escucho tu voz me siento llena con mucha emoción"*. She's happy when I call because it brings her joy to know that her grandkid still remembers her, and if you had a chance to make your grandparent happy wouldn't you take it?

On my desk, I keep pictures I took during my time in México with my *abuelos* for inspiration. I also have pictures of my friends from México. I look at them as I write, and it brings me back to this joy I found from the place my parents left behind. It makes me happy to see myself so full of joy, and I am so proud of myself for being the one courageous enough to follow her dreams despite any judgement or worry from others. It made me realize that anything is possible, that the courage I held in my heart, the overcoming of fear, and the openness of my heart brought not only joy for myself and the people I befriended but also the people I will share my story with. As I sit and look at these pictures, I realize the pride and joy that I held and reflect on how happy I was— not in a melancholic reminiscing kind of way but in a "this happiness is always in my reach, every day and every moment. It's just up to me!". To know that and hold that in my heart is probably the best lesson I have learned.

I'm sitting here crying, not out of sadness but out of joy that I was blessed enough to have lived a life I couldn't have ever dreamed of and with tremendous gratitude that I not only have this story but also the tools with which to share it with. People live extraordinary lives everywhere, but somehow, I was blessed with this message to be shared with anyone willing to read it and come along in this journey with me. That's who I wrote this book for: those who connect with my cultural upbringing, those who connect with a story of immigration, those who connect with a story of adventure and courage, those who connect with a journey of finding love within yourself. It is especially for those who, despite having looked everywhere for love, might be having a hard time finding it because, despite what you might think, the fact that you are out there looking means you're on the right path to finding it. Pursue your curiosity because that joy, that love you are searching for, is just on the other side of the fear holding you back from going after it.

I often think of my time in Playa del Carmen on the last couple of days before my adventure in México came to an end. I would be out walking the streets, loving the brown glow of my skin, the breeze flowing through my hair, and my tired cheeks as I had been smiling the entire time I was walking. I often wondered if people ever wonder what I'm smiling about because I would tell them I was smiling at life, and I hope that if they saw me smile they would smile too, and often they did. Laughter, joy, and love are contagious, and I want to continue living a life in that path. The lessons I have learned, especially that of exercising courage, have definitely led me in that path. I'm a free person, free to pursue what I want and not be afraid of it, and if I am afraid, I am now aware enough to know that if I listened to that fear I would be holding myself back. So to those who are reading this book that I so lovingly wrote, take that leap of faith in yourself. Let fear be your compass, and let courage be your guide, just like our parents did when they came to this country.

ACKNOWLEDGMENTS

One of my tíos reminded me that when I was younger and would visit México I would always come with a *maleta* filled with books. I had almost forgotten about that, but I do remember going to the library and checking out as many books as I could before heading out to México so I could read during the long drive and during my time there because there was no TV or internet. I've always had a love for books and writing a book was something I had on my bucket list, but I didn't actually know if and when I was going to make it happen. Now, here it is! In this journey I realized the importance of storytelling, it is a big part of our culture and we must tell our stories so they are not forgotten.

For this, I have to thank my family, especially my parents. Despite my crazy adventures and not fully understanding my reasons, they remained supportive through all my journeys. I realized that they would rather see me happy than just successful, and through this journey, I managed to be both. To my nieces and nephews, who remind me of the importance of passing down all that I have learned and who with their innocent hearts remind me that a tickle war and a pillow fight are often necessary to get through life. To my siblings, *primas*, *primos*, *tías*, and *tíos*, may we continue to share and reminisce about what brings us together and makes us who we are, *familia*.

To my tribe of friends who continuously checked in on me and shared meals, company, and conversation. Special thanks to my dear friend Siomara, who from the beginning reminded me there are kind people everywhere in our travels and who opened up her home to me upon my return and was supportive during this whole writing process, who would cook and share meals with me and comforted me when she found me crying as I wrote these chapters. And most importantly for sharing Bacon, the most handsome Labrador, who kept me company and brought me so much joy while I wrote this book.

To Gloria Felix who illustrated the beautiful cover and incorporated all the beautiful things of our Michoacán culture. A fellow Michoacana herself who came to the U.S. to pursue her masters degree in visual development and now focuses her art on representing our culture.

To my rancho and my beloved México and all the people in it who shared their company, their stories, their laughter, and even a dance with me. To all my new friendships that will last a lifetime, and to all the special memories I will hold in my heart. To all the strangers who are now friends and reminded me of the importance of relying on kindness.

Finally, to my *abuelos* who loved me unconditionally just as I am. *Los quiero mucho a todos!*

ABOUT THE AUTHOR

Maira Hernández is a first-generation Mexican American who was raised in an urban neighborhood in Los Angeles by immigrant parents. She was taught that education was the path to success, and after graduating from UC Berkeley, she realized her heart was in serving the community. Throughout her career, Maira has been an advocate for education but more so career success for marginalized individuals. She has mentored and coached first-generation students and young professionals on how to leverage their education, skills and knowledge to step into better opportunities.

In her work, Maira has recognized the effects of imposter syndrome, especially in high achieving individuals who suffer from burnout in the workplace environment. She works to inspire her community to continue growing and to continue making positive changes towards diversity while at the same time taking care of themselves. She strives to help people find empowerment by reconnecting to their culture, values and heritage that their motherlands provide and by helping them implement lessons from the motherland in their daily lives.

Having worked for non-profits guiding students through

higher education and recognizing the need for cultural empowerment she decided to go on her very own *Eat, Pray, Love* adventure with a Mexican twist. In *Aventura, Amor y Tacos,* she shares the greatness that runs through her ancestry in order to help others discover their own.

GRACIAS!

Con todo mi corazón, thank you so much for reading *Aventura, Amor y Tacos— The Path to Reconnecting with the Motherland*! If you've made it through this journey, I know you are more ready than ever to go on your own adventure, whether that entails a trip back to the motherland or doing it from the comfort of your own home. That adventure is waiting for you!

Pero, te diste cuenta? Did you notice? All of my chapters are named after some of the most common *dichos* and classic Mexican songs. Every single one of those phrases holds so much wisdom that has been passed down from generation to generation. You might have even heard them before from one of your elders. Share a memory, share a *dicho,* or your favorite song with me!

There is so much wisdom in the words our elders share with us. Let us use that wisdom as a source of empowerment to keep moving forward. As children of immigrants we inherit strength, will-power, perseverance, courage, and the capacity to dream and dream big!

Join me in exploring our own ancestry through the lens of

our own families so we can tap into all of the amazing gifts our elders have given us through stories of inheritance. Join me in The RAICES Society on Facebook as we share these stories, wisdoms, recipes, and pictures of the places we originate from and the lessons and insights you have gained in your own exploratory adventure of getting to know your own personal heritage.

And if you get the chance to visit your motherland, I would love for you to share your adventures. Keep in touch on Instagram, share your pictures, and share your stories, and visit www.mairahernandez.com for more resources and a free guide on how to get started and implement these lessons in your daily life to reconnect with your motherland.

REFERENCE

It was important for me to keep the language of this book as authentic to my daily life and that of many bilingual speakers who so commonly use Spanglish. With that in mind, I created a reference page for non-Spanish speakers to reference words commonly found in the book especially those who have cultural references specific to México.

Chapter 1
Si Se Puede! - Yes We Can!

Chapter 2
No Mas Recorriendo El Mundo
Just Traveling the World

Chapter 3
Ojos Que No Ven, Corazón Que No Siente
Out of Sight, Out of Mind

꧁꧂

A

Abuelos- Grandparents

Adobe- A building constructed from clay or sun-dried bricks

Atole- A traditional hot corn and masa beverage

B

Baile- A dance party, often to celebrate a milestone like a wedding or quinceañera or following a town's patron fiestas or rodeos

Banda- A style of Regional Mexican music composed of an ensamble of brass, percussion, and wind instruments.

Barro- Clay

Bendición- Blessing, often given by mothers in the form of the sign of the cross to bless someone's departure.

Bisabuelos- Great-grandparents

C

Calavera- Skeleton

Caldo de Pollo- Chicken Soup

Caña- Sugar cane

Cancha- Basketball Court

Canela- Cinnamon

La Capilla- The Chapel

Cariño- Affection

Carnitas- A dish of Mexican cuisine originating from Michoacán made by braising or simmering pork in lard until tender.

Carretera- Highway

Cebollitas- Type of firework popular in México that let's out sparks and spins when lit.

Cempasúchil- Mexican marigolds often used for Día de Los Muertos Celebrations

La Cena- Dinner

Cerro- Hill

Chancla- A sandal often associated with a Latin kid getting a spanking.

Chilaquiles- Traditional Mexican dish made of crisp tortillas and salsa.

Chile- Chili Peppers

Chisme- Gossip

Colcha- Bedspread

Comal- Smooth and flat griddle typically used to cook tortillas, toast spices and nuts, etc

La Comida- Afternoon Lunch, usually served around 3:00 pm.

Comunidad- Community

Corridos- A popular Mexican narrative song in a form of a ballad.

D

Desayuno- Breakfast

E

Enchiladas- A Mexican dish consisting of a corn tortilla rolled around a filling and covered with chili pepper sauce.

F

Fiestas- Celebrations in Mexican towns celebrating religious and cultural traditions.

Frijoles- Beans

G

Gazpacho- Fruit salad with origins in Michoacán made

of chopped mango, pineapple, jicama, and orange juice and powdered chili and often topped with cheese.

Gringo- A person, especially an American, who is not Hispanic or Latino.

Guares- Woman dressed in traditional Purépecha attire, wearing embroidered blouse, a heavy flowing skirt and braids in her hair.

Gusgueras- Junk Food

H

Huaraches- Traditional Mexican leather sandals, originally worn by Mexican natives.

Huevos- Eggs

I

La India María- One of the most popular characters in Mexican TV and film, a humble and stubborn indigenous woman portrayed by María Elena Velasco.

J

Jacal- Adobe-style housing structure

L

Leña- Firewood
Lonjas- Love handles, fat rolls
Lujo- Luxury
Lumbrada- Bonfire

M

Maleta- Luggage

El Mandado- Errands, food and supplies needed for the day often purchased in a pueblo or bigger town.

La Mordida- A Mexican tradition during birthday parties where the person who's birthday it is has to take a bite of the cake while someone smashes their face as they are taking a bite leaving them covered in frosting.

Mariachi- Traditional Mexican folk music with string instruments and trumpets performed by musicians dressed in native costumes.

Metate- A flat or slightly hollowed stone tool used to grind grain and seeds using another stone, often used to grind maize for tortillas.

Mocosa- Snotty-nosed, often when crying or sick

Molcajete- Traditional Mexican version of the mortar used for grinding various food products.

N

Nixtamal- The process for the preparation of maize in which the corn is soaked and cooked in an alkaline solution, usually limewater.

El Norte- The North often used to reference the U.S.

Nuez- Pecan

O

Ofrenda- Offering

P

Paletero- Ice cream man

Pan Dulce- Mexican sweet bread

Panteón- Cemetery

Parcelas- A plot of land, typically referring to the agricultural plots where crops are grown

Pesos- Mexican Currency

Piña- Pineapple

Platica- Chatting

Plaza- Town square

Plazuela- Small square near the town plaza

Posadas- Religious tradition celebrated largely in Latin

America commemorating the journey that Joseph and Mary made in search of safe refuge for the birth of baby Jesus. Celebrated for nine days before Christmas the town goes from house to house praying, singing, and sharing goods at the end of the gathering.

Pozole- Traditional Mexican hominy soup often seasoned with chili peppers and garnished with cabbage or lettuce, onions, cilantro, radish and avocado.

Primos- Cousins

Pueblo- Small towns in Mexico often bigger in population than a rancho.

Pueblo Mágico- Magical Towns in México

Purépecha- Indigenous people in the region of Michoacán.

Q

Quebradita- Mexican dance style meaning "little break" performed to banda music.

Quinceañera- Latin American tradition for a young girl turning fifteen and transitioning from childhood to young womanhood.

R

Rancheras- Traditional Mexican folk music often sung by mariachis.

The Rancho- A small ranch town in México where agriculture and farm life is most prominent. People refer to "the rancho" when talking about their own place of origin, which for different people can mean different towns.

Rebozo- A long scarf used to cover the head and shoulders traditionally worn my Mexican women.

S

Sopa De Vaso- Cup O'Noodles

Spanglish- The mix of Spanish and English, often used by Latinos in the U.S.

T

Tamales- Traditional Mesoamerican dish made of corn masa or dough steamed in corn husks

Tamborazo- A band of instrumental musicians, closely related to brass banda.

Tejana- Cowboy hat

Tía/Tío- Aunt/Uncle

Tiendita- Small corner store in the town where limited amount of goods can be bought including snacks and household items.

Tierra Mojada- Wet earth

Los Toros- The rodeo were the town gathers to watch bull-riding.

Torta- Mexican sandwich

Traviesos- Troublemakers

V

La Virgen de Guadalupe- The Virgin Mary

Visita- Visiting guests

Z

Zapateado- Dance style of Mexico, characterized by a lively rhythm punctuated by the striking of the dancer's shoes.

Zarape- A brightly colored shaw/blanket fringed at the ends popular in Mexico.

Made in the USA
Coppell, TX
01 November 2019

10782684R00076